Contents

Plot synopsis   4

Who's who in *Emma*   7

Themes, images and language in *Emma*   12

Text commentary Volume 1   22

Self-test questions Volume 1   31

Text commentary Volume 2   32

Self-test questions Volume 2   42

Text commentary Volume 3   43

Self-test questions Volume 3   56

How to write a coursework essay   58

How to write an examination essay   61

Self-test answers   65

■ Plot synopsis

Emma Woodhouse, mistress of Hartfield, the most substantial house in Highbury, Essex, seems to have everything she could want. In reality, however, her existence is rather narrow and dreary. Her mother is dead, her married sister lives in London and her father is an elderly hypochondriac who cannot provide her with companionship. When we first meet Emma, her life has been further diminished by the marriage of her governess, Miss Taylor, who has loved and indulged Emma for many years.

Miss Taylor's new husband is Mr Weston, a kindly and energetic man who has improved his fortune through his own efforts. He has a son, Frank Churchill, who has taken the name of his snobbish and autocratic uncle and aunt. The Churchills adopted him on the death of his mother, who had been disowned on her marriage to Mr Weston.

Chief amongst the Woodhouses' acquaintance in the area is Mr Knightley, who owns most of Highbury and the entire parish of Donwell, where he lives in Donwell Abbey. Mr Knightley is the elder brother of Emma's brother-in-law and has known her all her life. Mr Knightley is the only person who can see faults in Emma, but they enjoy a friendly, teasing relationship.

Emma fills the void left by Miss Taylor by forming a friendship with Harriet Smith, a beautiful but rather naïve girl who, because she is illegitimate, lives at Mrs Goddard's school. Harriet is starting to fall in love with Robert Martin, a local farmer and a protégé of Mr Knightley, but Emma feels this is an unworthy match for Harriet. She decides to do some matchmaking, and does all she can to throw Harriet into the arms of Mr Elton, the young Vicar of Highbury.

Emma's first strategy is to draw Harriet's portrait, which Emma believes will focus Mr Elton's attention on her friend's beauty. Mr Elton, however, is interested in the artist rather than the sitter. Mr Knightley chastises Emma for encouraging Harriet to turn down Robert Martin's proposal.

Emma's next move is to encourage her young friend to make a collection of charades or riddles in order to give Mr Elton an excuse to make a declaration. She assumes that the poem he offers for the collection is intended for Harriet. By December, Emma is becoming desperate to finalise her wedding plans for Harriet and to prove Mr Knightley wrong. She pretends to break her bootlace in order to get Harriet inside the Vicarage. Her disappointment at the failure of this move is forgotten when her sister and brother-in-law arrive with their little boys to celebrate Christmas at Hartfield.

Emma laughs off John Knightley's warnings that Mr Elton is in love with her, but he is proved right when the family go to dinner at Mr Weston's house and Mr Elton proposes to Emma in the carriage on the way home in the snow. Emma now faces the prospect of breaking the news to Harriet and resolves to give up matchmaking forever. This is a resolve that she soon breaks. Although Emma had begun to toy with the idea of marrying Frank Churchill herself (a secret wish of the Westons, in spite of the fact that the two have never met) she now begins to plan his marriage to Harriet. Mr Knightley, in the meantime, begins to express an apparently unreasonable dislike of Frank Churchill.

Jane Fairfax arrives in Highbury to stay with her grandmother, Mrs Bates. Jane is an orphan and has been living with the wealthy Campbell family as a companion for the young Miss Campbell. However, her friend has recently married and Jane now faces the prospect of earning her living as a governess. Emma dislikes Jane, who is clever, elegant and accomplished. News arrives of Mr Elton's engagement to a Miss Hawkins whom he met in Bath.

Distraction from Emma's concerns about Harriet arrives in the form of Frank Churchill. He is a lively and amusing young man who encourages Emma to speculate about a possible liaison between Jane Fairfax and Mr Dixon, the husband of the former Miss Campbell.

Gossip about Frank Churchill's visit to London for a haircut is eclipsed by gossip about a piano, delivered to Jane Fairfax by an anonymous donor. Frank encourages Emma to believe it is a gift from Mr Dixon. Meanwhile, Mrs Weston begins to believe that Mr Knightley is falling in love with Jane. As Frank Churchill's visit continues, he endears himself to all by making calls on the Bates family and planning a ball in the Crown Inn. Unfortunately, he is recalled to Yorkshire before the ball can take place. As he leaves, he seems on the point of making a declaration of love to Emma.

The return of the newly married Mr Elton to Highbury prompts a number of social events, which dissipate the gloom caused by Frank's departure. Mrs Elton proceeds to patronise Jane Fairfax.

When Frank's return is announced, the plan for the ball is taken up again. At the ball, Harriet is snubbed by Mr Elton, but Mr Knightley dances with her and then with Emma. When Frank rescues Harriet from gypsies the following day, Emma believes he is ready to fall for Harriet. The social round continues with a strawberry picking party at Donwell Abbey, but the day ends with fractured tempers. A trip to Box Hill ends even more badly. Mr and Mrs Elton show open resentment of Emma and prompt her to flirt outrageously with Frank. She brings the visit to a close by insulting Miss Bates and travels home in tears after a reprimand from Mr Knightley. When Emma calls on Miss Bates to apologise, she discovers that Jane has decided to take up a post as governess.

The sudden news of Mrs Churchill's death has no sooner reached Highbury than Mrs Weston breaks even more astounding news to Emma. Frank Churchill and Jane Fairfax have been engaged since they met in Weymouth the previous autumn. He has been apparently courting Emma to hide his true relationship with Jane. She now faces the prospect of comforting Harriet for the second time.

When Emma breaks the news to Harriet, she is shocked to learn that the girl does not care for Frank. Harriet is in love with Mr Knightley. Emma is devastated because she now realises that she herself has been in love with Mr Knightley all the time. Believing her to be grieving for Frank, Mr Knightley comes to comfort Emma. When she tells him she has never loved Frank, Mr Knightley proposes to her. Harriet's disappointment is the one cloud on Emma's horizon, so she sends Harriet to stay in London. Once there, Harriet meets up with Robert Martin and immediately accepts his proposal of marriage. The novel ends with news of the three marriages.

Emma

Emma Woodhouse is presented to us at the opening of the novel as the most fortunate of beings. She is happy, healthy, wealthy, intelligent and good looking. In the course of the novel, we revise some of these assumptions about Emma. By the end of the novel she has learned to accept that Mr Knightley has been right to warn her about the way she treats others. Austen describes Emma as an 'imaginist'. It is her vivid imagination that leads to the problems she creates when she attempts to make matches between people. As we learn more about her life, we realise that her imagination is her refuge from a rather dull and lonely existence, which is made difficult by her father's invalidism.

Another refuge is her pride in her social position. If she is lonely, she can at least console herself that she is not looking for companionship amongst the unworthy. We see Emma revising her ideas about who is acceptable and who is not and learning to be less snobbish. Austen is very careful to place her precisely in her social position. Her family has wealth and is long established at Hartfield but, with regard to landed property, they are not the equals of the Knightley family who own most of the two parishes of Highbury and Donwell. In her marriage to Mr Knightley, Emma will gain social standing as well as a reliable moral guide.

Emma has a contradictory attitude to marriage. She is fascinated by the thought of arranging marriages for others, but claims not to want marriage for herself. As a wealthy heiress, Emma is the only one of the main female characters who is in a position to make such a decision.

Mr Knightley

The very name 'Knightley' suggests this character's moral superiority. He is the character who can most often be relied upon to behave well. He ignores the social barriers that stand between him and Robert Martin or William Larkin and yet is considerate and gentle in taking care not to offend the Bates family. Mr Knightley might be said to represent all the traditional English country values. The adjectives used by Emma to describe Donwell Abbey also describe its owner. He is 'respectable', 'suitable' and 'becoming'. Like his house with its 'many comfortable and one or two handsome rooms', Mr Knightley is not so grand as to be off-putting, but has a solid background of good breeding.

His one failing is the jealousy that leads him to be overcritical of Frank Churchill, although this criticism is often justified. His finest hour is when he rescues Harriet from the ignominy of being cut by Mr Elton at the ball. His reward for this is that his participation in the dance alerts Emma to his existence as a sexual being who might be considered as a potential partner and not a brother.

Rather like Emma, Mr Knightley seems detached from his feelings in the early chapters of the novel and seems too comfortable in the role of bachelor uncle to be suitable husband material. As we see him take to the dance floor with Harriet and become the subject of village gossip when his name is connected with that of Jane Fairfax we, like Emma, begin to realise he has something to offer. The fact that Mr Knightley changes and grows and has small faults makes him a fully rounded character who is realistically human, rather than being a sanctimonious do-gooder.

Emma adopts a rather teasing attitude to Mr Knightley for most of the novel, possibly to defend herself from his blaming and lecturing. She teases him as a younger sister would an older brother. Once their relationship becomes that of husband and wife, she is prepared to accept his moral guidance.

Jane Fairfax

Because Jane is the same age as Emma, everyone in Highbury compares the two young women. This is, of course, what the reader is invited to do as well. Both women are blessed with youth, beauty and intelligence but, while Emma is an independent heiress, Jane is the poor dependent of the Campbell family who took her in.

While Emma can be haughty and proud, Jane is forced to accept the rather pushy friendship of Mrs Elton. In adversity, Jane finds it easier to accept the sympathy of Mrs Cole than that of Emma, who has scorned her aunt. Although both women are equal in intelligence, Jane is Emma's superior when it comes to music. This seems to be a reflection of Jane's steady approach to all she does. Emma takes up and drops hobbies before she can develop her skills.

In personality, the two women are very different. Emma is impulsive and talkative, while Jane is quiet and reserved, and her only impulsive action is to agree to a secret engagement to Frank. This decision is the cause of her subsequent loss of control in the closing stages of the novel. Because of this, and also because she is kept off stage for so long, it is perhaps as difficult for the reader as it is for Emma to warm to Jane. She is at her most interesting when her feelings are aroused: when she denounces the hiring of governesses as the sale 'of human intellect', when she rushes home alone from Donwell Abbey or when she paces up and down in her bedroom after breaking off her engagement. By keeping Jane in the background and playing down her attractive qualities, Jane Austen helps us to grow to like her rather problematic heroine, Emma. We appreciate her warmth and come to like her in spite of her faults.

Frank Churchill

At the end of the novel, readers may be left wondering what to make of Frank Churchill. His behaviour sometimes seems to fall below the high standard Austen sets for most of her sympathetic characters. Frank's easy good humour and rather careless treatment of Jane and Emma is reminiscent of Henry Crawford in *Mansfield Park*, although his transgressions are far less serious. When judging characters such as Frank Churchill or Henry Crawford, who share a rather ambiguous approach to right and wrong, it is useful to remember that Jane Austen is not a draconian judge of human behaviour: she can accept minor misdemeanours in likeable characters. Both Mr Weston and his son, Frank, bear some resemblance to Austen's brother, Henry. Because of his adoption by wealthy relatives, Frank also resembles another of Austen's brothers, Edward. Both brothers were well loved by their younger sister. Henry Austen was first a soldier and then a banker. When he went bankrupt he became a clergyman. He was married twice. The first marriage was to a cousin who was the widow of a French aristocrat who died at the guillotine. The couple enjoyed a sophisticated and pleasure-loving lifestyle. Frank's plans to cover Jane in his aunt's jewels might well have been inspired by this extravagant brother. Henry was not always totally reliable as his bankruptcy suggests, but he was much loved by everyone. Jane Austen's attitude to her brother is suggested by a comment in a letter, 'What a Henry!' She would probably expect us to have the same reaction to Frank.

Harriet Smith and Robert Martin

Harriet Smith and Robert Martin come from a different social background to the other pairs of lovers. Although Jane is poor she is well educated and has moved in cultured circles. Harriet is a pleasant but dull and ordinary girl made interesting by Emma's over-active imagination. Emma must learn to forget her romantic daydreams about the possibilities of Harriet's background when the mundane truth is revealed. Conversely, she must drop her snobbish attitude to Robert Martin who is a valued confidant of Mr Knightley.

Harriet's indecisive and impressionable nature serves to illuminate the theme of illusion and delusion. Emma is deluded as to the real intentions of Mr Elton, Frank Churchill and even Mr Knightley, but she is by no means as gullible as Harriet.

Robert has many of the solid virtues embodied by Mr Knightley and stands in relation to him very much as Abbey-Mill Farm does to Donwell Abbey. The great house stands at the edge of a steep bank: 'at the bottom of this bank, favourably placed and sheltered, rose the Abbey-Mill Farm.' In marrying Robert, Harriet will prosper and improve her social standing.

Mr and Mrs Elton

Mr and Mrs Elton are comic characters whom Austen uses to satirise the evils of snobbery. Although they are both snobs and we dislike them equally, their characters are carefully differentiated: each has his or her own particular awfulness. Mr Elton's snobbery takes the form of social climbing. In order to get on he tries to please everyone superior to himself. John Knightley comments, 'I never in my life saw a man more intent on being agreeable than Mr Elton. It is downright labour to him where ladies are concerned.' The insincerity of his flattery is highlighted by his refusal to dance with Harriet at the ball.

Mrs Elton's snobbery takes the form of boasting about her connections and contriving to take first place in all social gatherings. Her personality is far more abrasive than that of her husband and she influences him to sneer at Emma after their marriage. In satirising the Eltons, Austen makes clear her views on social pretension and we understand that, while Emma's snobbery is not to be approved of, it is less reprehensible than the Eltons'.

Themes, images and language in *Emma*

Wit and irony

Wit and irony

It is difficult to appreciate *Emma* to the full without having an appreciation of Austen's use of irony. A full range of ironic techniques is used in the novel. One of the most frequently used is ironic statement. In Chapter 1 we are told that Emma 'had lived nearly twenty-one years in the world with very little to distress or vex her.' We are not intended to take this statement at face value. As the chapter continues, we realise that Emma's life is made difficult by her father's hypochondria and his stay-at-home ways. Similarly, Mrs Goddard's school is described as a place 'where girls might be sent to be out of the way and scramble themselves into a little education, without any danger of coming back prodigies.' By this we are to understand that the school does not provide a good standard of education. Austen is not inviting us to agree that education is a thing to be avoided, she is satirising those who think that educating girls is a waste of time.

Some of the main characters make use of ironic statements in their conversation. John Knightley's rather caustic attitude is conveyed when he comments on the snow that may prevent them from returning home safely from the Christmas party at Randalls: ' "I admired your resolution very, much sir," said he, "in venturing out in such weather . . . I admired your spirit." ' He does no such thing, of course. By now we all understand that Mr Woodhouse, whom he is addressing, does not have the resolution of a new-born babe. Politeness dictates that John Knightley cannot openly attack his father-in-law, he can only resort to sarcasm.

Austen makes use of ironic impersonation to satirise Mrs Elton, a deeply unsympathetic character. At the dinner held in her honour at Hartfield, she discusses her clothes with Jane Fairfax. At first she says, 'But I am quite in the

12

minority, I believe; few people seem to value simplicity of dress,' implying that she herself is a paragon of quiet good taste. Her next comments, however, reveal that really, she tends towards ostentation and gaudy show: 'I have some notion of putting such trimming such as this to my white and silver poplin.' Her showy dress sense is also revealed by her comments about Emma's wedding. Ironic impersonation is achieved when a character such as Mrs Elton tries to give one impression but reveals the truth behind the pretence.

Miss Bates is another source of ironic impersonation but here the technique is used to quite different effect. Miss Bates slips away from the ball in order to see her elderly mother safely to bed; she says, 'I ran home, as I said I should, to help Grandmamma to bed, and got back again and nobody missed me. – I set off without a word,' but, of course, she finds it impossible to return without a word and gives a verbatim account of everything she and Mrs Bates said, which anyone might over-hear. Here, the effect produced is not to mock Miss Bates, as is the case with Mrs Elton; rather, we are led to admire her simple good-heartedness as she cheerfully breaks off from her evening's pleasure to attend to her elderly mother.

Another effect of irony is to distance the author from the characters; it is not immediately obvious with whom Austen sympathises and whom she dislikes. The reader has to read between the lines.

A further distance is created by Austen's use of wit. Many ideas are delivered in the form of finely turned aphorisms (brief, pithy remarks) or epigrams (concise and pointed or sarcastic remarks), and Austen's exact stance on a particular matter is often concealed by humour. The openings of chapters are a favourite place for such sayings. Chapter 22 begins, 'Human nature is so well disposed towards those who are in interesting situations, that a young person, who either marries or dies, is sure of being kindly spoken of.' What Austen is really saying is that the only reason why anyone would take a polite interest in Augusta Hawkins is because she is about to be married. This interpretation is borne out by the fact that all of the main characters heartily dislike her by the end of the novel. There is also a hint that Austen is equating marriage with death, something that suggests a much darker view of life than we might expect from such an apparently light-hearted and witty novelist.

Epigrams and aphorisms are also placed in the mouths of two of the main characters, to establish them as witty and intelligent. Emma rebukes Mr Knightley when he suggests Harriet should have accepted Robert Martin's proposal by saying, 'A man always imagines a woman to be ready for anybody who asks her.' This is very true of the plight of many of the women in the novel, whose only escape from a life of poverty is matrimony. Emma, however, overlooks the fact that Harriet literally is ready to marry anyone who asks her and so the effect of this aphorism is to make Emma seem over-confident about her ability to judge the character of others. When Mr Knightley resorts to an epigram, he is able to do so with greater insight. He says of Emma's friendship with Harriet, 'Her [Harriet's] ignorance is hourly flattery.' The perception of this statement is enhanced by the witty apposition of the words 'ignorance' and 'flattery' around the word 'is'.

Love and marriage

Love and marriage

Every one of Austen's novels centres on the subject of love and marriage, each novel ending with at least one wedding. In *Emma*, Jane Austen seems to be exploring what makes for a good relationship. She shows that marriage is the only possible refuge for a woman without fortune, and a refuge from loneliness.

We are presented with a number of different marriages and invited to make comparisons. The first couple to marry is Mr and Mrs Weston. Their happy marriage reflects the good-humoured and generous personalities of the two people involved. It is in sharp contrast to the unhappy marriage of Mr and Mrs Churchill, dominated by the spiteful self-centredness of the wife, who poisons the lives of all her near relatives. Each couple gives us an example of the importance of goodwill in a small and closely-knit society. The good-natured hospitality of the Westons is an asset to Highbury society, with Mr Weston organising balls and outings for his friends. The snobbish cold-heartedness of Mrs Churchill is a barrier to social intercourse: she acts twice as a barrier to courtship and effectively postpones the ball planned by Frank and Emma.

John and Isabella give us a picture of a marriage that is adapting to accommodate young children. John Knightley is a loving father who a takes his young sons for walks and accompanies them on visits. Much of his irritability is caused by events that encroach on time spent with his family. He is an affectionate man whose sensibility makes him the first to spot Mr Elton's true intentions towards Emma and gives him an insight into Jane's sadness. Isabella has never been as intelligent as Emma – she is portrayed as being totally wrapped up in her children and only able to view events as they affect her children.

The Eltons are well matched and agree on most things. Unfortunately, the main things they have in common are their snobbery and affectation. This means that their marriage is built on the shaky foundation of pretence. As Frank Churchill says at Box Hill, 'How well they suit each other!'

The main focus of the novel is on the courtships of Jane Fairfax and Frank Churchill, Harriet Smith and Robert Martin and Emma and Mr Knightley. Emma and Mr Knightley play the principal roles. The constantly shifting pairings emphasise the difficulty of finding the right partner. Harriet rejects Robert Martin only to realise he is the man for her. Emma finds true love not with Frank Churchill, the interesting new arrival, but with Mr Knightley who has always been a part of her life. Jane continues to love Frank despite the mistreatment she has to endure from him.

We are led to reflect on what makes a good partnership. Robert Martin's steadiness will counteract Harriet's inability to know her own mind. Jane Fairfax's decorum and good sense will balance her future husband's impetuosity. Mr Knightley's good sense will put a brake on Emma's overactive imagination. If Mr Knightley is a little dull compared with the dashing Frank Churchill, he is at least reliable.

The time of courtship is realistically portrayed as a time of danger and even anguish. Joy comes only once a number of difficulties have been resolved. For Jane and Harriet, marriage is shown to be the only real escape from a life of financial insecurity. It is possible to work as a governess and be happy, as the example of Miss Taylor proves; old age, however, brings insurmountable difficulties, as we see in the case of Miss Bates. The women of the novel share this difficulty with lower-class men, such as John Abdy, who must resort to seeking help from the parish. Quite clearly, economics as well as gender create the difficulties the women face.

Given that the stakes are high, courtship is portrayed as a time when careful choices are to be made. Harriet risks losing her best chance of a happy marriage. Jane wonders if she has made a hasty decision in agreeing to marry Frank after only a brief acquaintance. Mr Elton's proposal to Emma serves to warn her of the dangers of giving off the wrong signals in the marriage market. It is not a lesson she profits from as she goes on to make a similar mistake when she openly flirts with Frank Churchill at Box Hill.

Courtship holds dangers for men as well as women – one has only to consider the fate of Mr Churchill senior to realise this. Mr Knightley becomes aware of the damage that can be inflicted on tender feelings and returns with relief 'to the coolness and solitude' of his bachelor home. At the end of the novel, however, we are given the conventional view of marriage being the happy culmination of courtship.

Illusion and delusion

Illusion and delusion

Despite the fact that the action of *Emma* is entirely set within the small society of Highbury and Donwell, where everybody knows and discusses everybody else's business, this is a novel about the difficulty involved in understanding and interpreting the actions of others. Although the neighbours of Highbury live on top of each other, they do not really know each other.

Emma Woodhouse is one of the most intelligent women in the novel, and yet she misinterprets the actions of others at every turn. She believes Harriet to be the object of Mr Elton's affections and then of Frank Churchill's. When she thinks she is at her most perceptive, for instance when she believes she has uncovered an affair between Jane Fairfax and Mr Dixon, she is really completely deluded and the victim of Frank Churchill's deception.

Mr Knightley provides a benchmark for intelligence and good sense in the novel. He is the first to notice the relationship between Jane and Frank. But even he allows his jealousy to cloud his judgement when he over-reacts and allows his dislike of the young man to become obvious. His jealousy even blinds him to the fact that Emma is in love with him and not with Frank.

Mr and Mrs Weston experience their share of delusion as they fondly imagine that Frank will fall in love with and marry Emma. Frank, in his turn, deliberately creates illusions to cover up his engagement to Jane Fairfax.

The secret engagement between Frank Churchill and Jane Fairfax highlights the theme of illusion and delusion. The secret makes fools of everyone, even the reader who is put in the same position as most of the residents of Highbury. The novel is strewn with clues to their liaison that can only be interpreted and understood once the secret is out. Frank's letter to Mr and Mrs Weston and the final meeting between Emma, Frank and Jane are used to explain the significance of these clues.

Rank and status

Rank and status

A reader who is not familiar with Jane Austen's values or her ironic point of view might be tempted to dismiss her as a snob. This would be to misunderstand both her intentions within the novel and her views of morality.

Before examining Jane Austen's attitudes, it is useful to look at the society that influenced her. Jane Austen lived at a time when great changes were taking place and a previously rigidly structured society was becoming more fluid and subject to change. Her own family provides examples of this, as do the characters of her novels. Her brother Edward moved up in society due to the old influence of patronage when wealthy relatives adopted him. Frank Churchill benefits from similar advantages. Her other brothers, however, made their own fortunes in the army and the navy, as well as in the world of finance. It has already been pointed out that Mr Weston's career was similar to that of Henry Austen. Jane Austen's naval brothers prospered in the same way that Captain Wentworth and Admiral Croft in *Persuasion* did: by rising through the ranks and benefiting from bounty awarded when ships were captured from the French in the Napoleonic wars. The circulation of new money led, inevitably, to social change as new families achieved social status through the acquisition of wealth.

There are always some people who will resist change, and this is what we see taking place in *Emma*. The Churchills resist social change and attempt to exert their influence over two generations of the same family. Being weak and elderly, Mr Woodhouse also resists change and benefits from maintaining the *status quo*, as the Bates family and Mrs Goddard remain at his beck and call. The *nouveau riche* Cole family are anxious not to rock the boat or offend anyone with their new-found wealth, so they comply with the mores of an older society. They defer to the Woodhouse family and issue invitations to their guests in accordance with their social status. The important families are invited to dinner while lesser individuals join them when the meal is over. Mrs Elton, the social climber, apes her betters in everything, including their snobbery. If Mrs Elton is belittled by Austen for her connections with trade, the possibility that her brother-in-law was involved in the slave trade goes some way to explain this.

Initially Austen's ironic standpoint masks her real feelings about snobbery. When we look at the attitudes of sympathetic characters in the book, her views become clearer. Mr Knightley serves as a benchmark for good behaviour within the book. He has a democratic view of society. He views Robert Martin as a useful and valued confidant in agricultural matters and is to be found as often in the society of his employee William Larkin as others of higher rank. His regard for the Bates family takes their lower social status into account and he treats them all the more considerately because of it. While good feeling influences Mr Knightley's democratic attitude, the ebullience and sociability of Mr Weston and his son mean that they are also democratic. Mr Weston issues invitations to his ball to all and sundry; Frank makes an offer of marriage to Jane Fairfax who has no fortune or connections. When Emma considers teaching the Coles a lesson for being presumptuous, 'she had little hope of Mr Knightley, none of Mr Weston.'

In the course of the novel, Emma has to choose between adopting the snobbish and exclusive attitudes of the Churchills or learning democracy from Mr Knightley. In marrying Mr Knightley, she accepts she has been wrong to be snobbish. She realises that true worth does not come from social status or high rank, as Mrs Elton believes. Through watching Emma learn her lesson we realise that Austen believes that the real values of generosity and kindliness are accessible to all, whatever their social station. Gentility comes from within, not from social standing.

Narrative style and structure

The chief feature of the narrative of *Emma* is the fact that most events are viewed through Emma's eyes. This means we share in Emma's confusion and difficulty as she comes to terms with her inability to read the actions of others and realises that she is not as clever as she had thought. This serves to emphasise the impact of the theme of illusion and delusion, as we share in Emma's misreading of situations. Our identification with Emma is reinforced by the fact that her inner thoughts are often revealed to us, as they are after the proposal from Mr Elton.

Just as Emma is deluded by illusions of her own cleverness, other characters in the book are obsessed by their own preoccupations. Much of the humour of the book arises from the clash of interests as characters attempt to drag their own concerns into the conversation. This happens when Mr Weston tries to talk to Mrs Elton about his son, while her sole concern is to dwell on the glories of Maple Grove.

Further humour is derived from the way that misunderstandings lead to conversations held at cross-purposes. When Emma discusses Harriet's new love with her, Emma presumes Harriet to be in love with Frank Churchill, although the real object of the girl's affections is Mr Knightley. When Mr Knightley comes to see Emma after the revelation of Frank's engagement, he believes she is mourning a lost love, while Emma believes he is about to announce his love for Harriet. All confusion is happily resolved with Mr Knightley's proposal to Emma.

Although the plot of *Emma* concerns small events taking place in a small village, there is a good deal of tension and suspense. An initial source of suspense is the fact that two of the main characters remain off stage for so long. By the time we meet them, our curiosity about Frank and Jane has been considerably aroused. Our expectations of Mrs Elton are fairly negative once we fully understand the shallowness of her husband's character. Her arrival at Highbury is heralded by several mentions that arouse our curiosity, but her true awfulness is held back by Austen until our second meeting with her when her snobbish self-absorption is given full rein. The chief suspense arises when Emma believes that Mr Knightley may be in love with Harriet. The final climax of the novel comes as all the problems created by Emma's interference in Harriet's life are smoothed away.

Throughout the novel, regular references to the passing of the seasons and the changing weather provide a backdrop to the changes in partners, attitudes and moods. Austen seems to be suggesting that the world of nature can provide a constant point of reference in a changing world. Although seasons may change, they will return again. The novel begins and ends in the autumn. This serves to emphasise the circularity of the seasons, but also leads us to consider how much can change in one short year.

Imagery

Imagery

The main feature of Austen's style is her use of irony and humour. Apart from the complication of understanding her point of view, her style is transparent and makes little use of imagery. However, the cataclysmic effect of Emma's discovery that she loves Mr Knightley is emphasised by the rare use of an image as she realises 'with the speed of an arrow, that Mr Knightley must marry no one but herself!'

Austen also makes use of recurring motifs to highlight the themes of the novel. The shifting patterns of the dances at the Coles' dinner party and the ball reflect the changing partners in the courtships that Emma believes she is organising. The charades that Harriet collects, with their riddling questions, reflect the difficulties that Emma experiences in interpreting the actions of her friends. The word games played with Emma's nephews' alphabet letters hint at the way we have to struggle to find the meaning of other people's actions.

The importance of the weather in the structure of the novel has already been referred to. The weather also plays a part in creating atmosphere: during the strawberry picking party at Donwell Abbey the weather seems in tune with the mood of the characters. The weather is hot and the tempers of Frank and Jane also become heated. Austen also uses the weather to create mood as Emma mourns what she believes to be the loss of Mr Knightley's love – although it is summer, the weather becomes autumnal. This reminds us of the elegiac mood of the opening of the novel as Emma mourned the loss of Miss Taylor. As rescue approaches in the form of a proposal from Mr Knightley, the weather improves and the summer weather returns.

Examiner's tips

Examination

Coursework

These icons are used throughout the **Text commentary** to highlight key points in the text, provide advice on avoiding common errors and offer useful hints on thoroughly preparing yourself for coursework and examination essays on this novel.

■ Text commentary

Volume 1: Chapters 1–3

The first three chapters introduce the residents of Highbury: those of the first and second sets.

'Emma Woodhouse... seemed to unite some of the best blessings of existence...' Emma is introduced in Jane Austen's most slyly

Wit and irony

ironic style. At first, it seems likely we will agree with Austen that Emma is a heroine 'whom no one would like but myself'. The death of her mother is glossed over in an unsentimental fashion and the instances of Emma's good fortune – 'handsome, clever, and rich, with a comfortable home and happy disposition' – tempt us to dismiss her as a smug and

Emma

spoiled heiress. One word, however, that centrally poised 'seemed', prompts us to look below the surface and detect the faults in Emma's character and the difficulties of a life spent indulging a petulant and hypochondriac parent. As Emma struggles to reconcile her father to 'poor Miss Taylor's' marriage, we begin to sympathise with Emma. What arguments does she provide for her father to persuade him to accept Miss Taylor's marriage and how are they received?

Examination

A common topic for examination questions is Austen's attitude to Emma. Be sure to interpret her ironic comments carefully. See examination essay 2, page 64.

Mr Knightley breaks in on this mournful conversation with a literal breath of fresh air as he draws back from Mr Woodhouse's fire. How does Austen establish the season of the year at this point? How does it fit in with the mood that Austen has established? Mr Knightley comments ironically on 'what sort of joy you must both be feeling', and treats Emma with the kind of briskness we may have begun to think she deserves; but as she strives to save her father from the pain of hearing her criticised, we again sympathise with her.

The discussion of Miss Taylor's marriage concludes with a pronouncement from Mr Knightley on the importance of 'a home of her own' and 'a comfortable provision' for a woman of Miss Taylor's age. It is significant that it is at this point that Emma introduces her scheme for matchmaking. She is willing to plan for others what she is not ready to contemplate for herself.

Love and marriage

The history of Mr Weston's first marriage is now delivered with a good deal of irony. Just as his second wife has moved up the social scale through marriage, so did Mr Weston with his first, but with less happy results. When Miss Churchill married her energetic and cheerful soldier, her brother and sister-in-law 'threw her off with due decorum'. Initially we may imagine that Jane Austen is a snob herself and is condoning the behaviour of the Churchills. It seems possible,

Wit and irony

at first, that the marriage is described as 'an unsuitable connection' because Mr Weston has married outside his class. When he is described as having a 'warm heart and sweet temper', we realise that Austen is wholly on Mr Weston's side and has been satirising the couple who imagine that it is decorous to cast off a sister who has married a decent and honourable man. The description of the widower's feelings as he gave up his son to his in-laws is also ironically portrayed from the Churchills' point of view. The few scruples and 'some reluctance the widower-father may be supposed to have felt' precisely delineate their callous attitude. Mr Weston's cheerful nature is very similar to that of Jane Austen's favourite brother, Henry, and his career follows a similar path. It is highly unlikely that Austen wants us to share the Churchills' disapproval. His efforts to move up the social ladder by increasing his wealth are finally rewarded by a happy marriage.

At this point in the novel, Frank Churchill is kept firmly off stage, where he is to stay for some time. In his absence he is represented by his letter, which is described as 'handsome' several times.

Rank and status

Having been introduced to Mr Knightley, the Westons, Frank Churchill and Mr Elton, who have been carefully placed in their social positions, we are ready to meet a 'second set': Mrs and Miss Bates and Mrs Goddard. Are we meant to take this indication of the ladies' social standing at face value? Mrs Bates is the widow of a clergyman now fallen upon hard times, very much as Mrs Austen did when her husband died. When Jane Austen says that Miss Bates 'had no intellectual superiority to make atonement to herself, or frighten those who might hate her,' she may be thinking of her own position and that of her mother. When Austen's father retired and moved to Bath, his unmarried daughters, Jane and Cassandra, were not consulted. When he died the two women and their mother had to rely on the charity of Jane's elder brother. Jane Austen knew what it was to play an inferior role in society. The harshness of those words 'frighten' and 'hate' seem a far cry from the cosy, polite world that some people would have us believe Austen lived in. They seem to be a sign of the well-hidden anger, which fuelled her ironic and satiric point of view. Indeed, her sense of humour probably helped her to endure a difficult situation. Although Miss Bates does not have the intellectual and artistic gifts of her creator, she has sufficient wit to realise that people treated the Vicar's daughter differently to the way in which they now treat an impoverished spinster. How does Miss Bates' situation help us to appreciate the importance of making a good match?

We also meet Harriet Smith, whose illegitimacy reminds us that Austen is writing in the Regency period: a time of 'rakes' and 'roués'. It is also a reminder that Austen is well aware of the less genteel side of life. Notice that Harriet's illegitimacy does not preclude her friendship with the Woodhouse family. What attractions does she hold for Emma?

Chapters 4 and 5

The friendship between Emma and Harriet grows.

As their friendship grows, Emma is perturbed by Harriet's feelings for Robert Martin. On being cross-examined by Emma, Harriet willingly paints a

Love and marriage

romanticised, but rather touching portrait of the young farmer as he shares 'moonlight walks' with her, fetches walnuts for her and arranges for the shepherd's son to sing in the parlour. Such is the young man's devotion, he even promised to read *The Romance of the Forest* and *Children of the Abbey*, the kind of gothic novel satirised by Austen in *Northanger Abbey*. There is gentle humour in the description of Harriet's naïve conviction that the proximity of their birthdays has some propitious significance, and her consternation at the thought of Robert having to wait until he is thirty before marrying.

Illusion and delusion

Such is the impression that Robert Martin has on us when we view him through Harriet's eyes, that Emma's judgement of him comes as a shock: 'But a farmer can need none of my help, and is therefore in one sense as much above my notice as in every other he is below it.' Emma describes him as 'very plain' and feels his manners mark him out as 'a very inferior creature'. At this point in the novel Emma seems at her most cold and snobbish. She makes a comparison with Mr Elton which is unflattering to Robert Martin and to Mr Knightley, and begins her project of making a match between Mr Elton and Harriet. It might be expected that Emma would make an unfavourable contrast between Robert and Mr Elton, but what are we to make of the unfavourable comparison with Mr Knightley?

Emma

When Mr Knightley and Mrs Weston discuss the friendship between the two girls, our feeling that Emma may be being unfair to Robert Martin and to Harriet is confirmed. Mr Knightley sees Harriet's ignorance as a danger to Emma and recalls the fate of one of Emma's previous schemes – her reading list. What does this reveal about Emma's character? Mrs Weston's partial support of Emma is to be expected. Less expected, because of his criticism of her, are Mr Knightley's feelings towards Emma. He praises her looks and says he would 'like to see Emma in love' – he sows the thought in the reader's mind that Emma could fall in love. With a lightly humorous touch, Austen draws this conversation to a close just as it gets really interesting, with a discussion of the weather.

Chapter 6

Emma draws Harriet's portrait, and tries to encourage Mr Elton's interest in Harriet.

Wit and irony

In deciding to paint Harriet's portrait, Emma revives a hobby which, like the reading lists, had been long abandoned. Although she has begun the portrait to encourage Mr Elton's interest in Harriet, Emma soon tires of his fulsome praise of her handiwork, failing to notice that his attention is on the artist and not the sitter. Mr Knightley's comment, 'You have made her too tall,' is in comic contrast with Mr Elton's raptures, and emphasises his rational and sensible approach to life. Mr Woodhouse's response to the drawing is similarly revealing of his constant preoccupation – he worries about the girl in the portrait catching cold. By the end of the chapter, Emma is glad to pack Mr Elton and the portrait off to London. She has taken to mimicking his style of speech, 'Exactly so,' and cannot endure him, although she still considers him good enough for Harriet. What does this reveal about her attitude to Harriet?

Chapters 7 and 8

Harriet turns down an offer of marriage from Robert Martin and Mr Knightley rebukes Emma for her part in the refusal.

We receive a good indication of Harriet's real character in Chapter 7 as she

Love and marriage

quickly succumbs to the temptation of an offer from Robert Martin. Emma is called upon to use all her powers of persuasion to deter her young friend. She declares that such a marriage would mean an end to their friendship because of the social differences between the Martin family and herself. What other arguments does Emma produce to deter Harriet? She claims to be allowing Harriet to use her own discretion in

deciding what to do, but this is far from the truth. As usual, Emma is manipulating her friend. Some doubts begin to interfere with Emma's certainty that Robert Martin is an unworthy suitor when she is forced to admit to herself that his letter was 'much above her expectation'. These doubts are confirmed for the reader when Mr Knightley comes out strongly in defence of Robert in Chapter 8. It becomes clear that Mr Knightley has a much more democratic view of the young farmer, whom he regards as a trusted friend, and he has a far more realistic view of Harriet's marriage prospects.

Jane Austen encourages the reader to see everything from Emma's point of view, but here we are given a strong hint that she is not a reliable witness. Mr Knightley, however, with the insight born of greater maturity and a wider circle of acquaintance, can usually be trusted to judge a situation correctly, as

Narrative style and structure

when he says to Emma of Harriet 'your infatuation about that girl blinds you.' He has also seen a side of Mr Elton which has been concealed from Emma and, therefore, from the reader: 'From his general way of talking in unreserved moments, when there are only men present, I am convinced he does not mean to throw himself away.' Emma stubbornly refuses to be convinced even though she herself has tired of Mr Elton's

charms. Note that here we see Mr Elton through Mr Knightley's eyes. We are given a fleeting view of men talking alone – a rare occurrence in Austen's work.

Chapters 9 and 10

Emma continues to lure Mr Elton on Harriet's behalf.

Emma's grand scheme to educate and improve Harriet comes to nothing. Harriet's only literary occupation is a collection of riddles, which Emma soon uses as a trap for Mr Elton.

Austen uses the idea of riddles to great effect in this chapter. The difficulty that the characters experience in solving the riddles (especially Harriet and Mr Woodhouse) reflects the general difficulty that all the characters experience when they attempt to interpret the actions of others. Mr Woodhouse's contribution, with its repeated, 'Kitty, a fair but frozen maid,' serves to remind us of Emma's condition. She, who is so involved in the matrimonial adventures of others, seems to wish nothing for herself. Emma is very clever at solving riddles, but not so adept when it comes to the questions posed by real life.

Imagery

The chapter ends with Emma again complaining to herself about Mr Elton's ability to please, although she still continues to seek him out on behalf of her friend.

Examination

Keep a careful note of Austen's imagery in order to prepare for questions on narrative style. The humour produced by the characters' attempts to decipher the riddles is also noteworthy. See examination essay 1, page 63.

As she does throughout the novel, Austen makes a reference to the passing seasons and indicates that it is now mid-December. As Emma and Harriet walk in Vicarage-lane, how does the description of the Vicarage help to place Mr Elton in society? Emma speaks of her wish never to marry. She declares her intention of caring for her nephews and nieces in preference to any feelings that might be 'warmer and blinder'. Austen uses the reference to nieces to mention Jane Fairfax again, in order to keep this important character's name before us.

When Mr Elton appears, Emma quite literally stoops to a new low in her attempts to secure him for her friend. She pretends her shoelace is broken in order to prompt the ever-gallant Mr Elton to invite them both to the Vicarage. Although the hoped-for proposal is not forthcoming, Emma **Emma** feels pleased with her ruse. The reader is left wondering at her lapse in decorum. What impression have you formed, so far, of Jane Austen's views on decorum?

Chapters 11 and 12

John and Isabella arrive at Hartfield for Christmas.

The arrival of John and Isabella serves to distract both Emma and the reader

Narrative style and structure

from the pursuit of Mr Elton. Emma and Mr Knightley meet for the first time since they disagreed about Robert Martin. Isabella takes after her father, although it must be said in her favour that she is obsessed with the well-being of her children rather than herself. In the midst of the family conversation Frank Churchill is referred to once again. In the discussion of his letter, Weymouth and the date (September), are both

mentioned. These two facts are significant, as we will learn later. *Emma* is as full of clues and red herrings as any detective novel and you should try to keep track of them. Later, the name of Jane Fairfax crops up in the conversation; thus we are reminded again of these two absent characters.

As Isabella and her father discuss the relative merits of various watering places, Mr John Knightley becomes impatient when he hears his own health mentioned. What impression do we gain of the marriage of John and Isabella Knightley? Emma distracts him for a while with talk of a friend's estate. When he becomes impatient again it is Mr Knightley who distracts him, showing he had understood Emma's earlier intervention. Emma and Mr Knightley can work together despite their quarrel, and Mr Knightley is shown to be a source of support in Emma's problematic relationship with her father.

Chapters 13–15

The Woodhouses and the Knightleys dine with Mr and Mrs Weston.

Jane Austen prepares us for dinner at Randalls with great care. Harriet, who

Narrative style and structure

Emma

is ill, announces her intention of staying at home. John Knightley warns Emma that Mr Elton seems to be interested in her. As they compare notes on Harriet's illness, Emma cannot understand why Mr Elton is so cheerful. A threatened snowstorm is much discussed. Emma finds it difficult to cope with John Knightley's grumbles in the carriage. What do all these rather upsetting events seem to foreshadow? What effect is produced by the contrast between John Knightley and Mr Elton at this point?

When Emma arrives at Randalls, we are again reminded of the many petty irritations that plague Emma's life. She wishes to speak to Mrs Weston but has to be satisfied with 'her smile, her touch, her voice'. When Frank Churchill's name is mentioned, she is prevented from hearing more of this interesting topic because she is too polite to ask Mr Elton to stop talking. She is very angry with Mr Elton for preventing her from hearing more because she has begun to formulate a plan for marrying Frank Churchill. In what way do Frank Churchill's reasons for being unable to visit the Westons make him similar to Emma? How is Mrs Churchill similar to Mr Woodhouse? There is much discussion of Frank Churchill's predicament, which serves to make us eager to actually meet him. Yet again, Austen is forcing us to see things as Emma does.

Wit and irony

The next chapter is rich in irony as the realisation begins to dawn on Emma that Mr Elton is paying court to her. John Knightley uses ironic understatement and mock admiration to torment his father-in-law. Can you find these examples? In the panic that follows the discovery of the snow storm, only Mr Knightley keeps his head.

Emma finds herself alone with Mr Elton as the carriage takes them home. The proposal itself is rushed over in Austen's inimitable form of reported

Narrative style and structure

speech, 'hoping – fearing – ready to die if she refused him'. We are alerted to the suddenness of this attack by Austen's use of the passive form of the verb, 'she found her subject cut up – her hand seized – her attention demanded.' We are presented with the end result of Mr Elton's actions rather than being given a full description of his approach to Emma. We are left with the impression that she finds herself completely under siege almost before she even realises the attack has begun.

Examination

Some examination questions require candidates to give a close reading of a passage from the text. The details given above about style would be useful for such an answer. See examination essay 1, page 63.

Love and marriage

In contrast to the swiftness of the proposal, Emma takes several pages to turn him down. She has to endure the irony of hearing her own argument against Robert Martin now used against Harriet, 'Everybody has their level'. She is forced to realise that all the wiles used to catch Mr Elton for her friend have convinced him that there was reason to believe that Emma would accept his offer. When she succeeds in rejecting him, they are forced to continue their journey in mortified silence. A final irony comes when a newly cheerful John Knightley welcomes a dejected Emma home.

Chapters 16 and 17

Emma recovers her dignity and comforts Harriet.

Illusion and delusion

Emma is upset by the overthrow of her plans and insulted by Mr Elton's proposal, but her chief concern is for Harriet. When she looks back over previous weeks, she realises 'it was all confusion'. She reflects that only the Knightley brothers had a true notion of Mr Elton's character. At first, Emma is tempted to blame Mr Elton's inferior background for the fact that he believed he had grounds for so presumptuously proposing to her. Gradually, however, she admits to herself that she had also misinterpreted Mr Elton's feelings and her own behaviour had been over 'complaisant and obliging'. She tells herself she was wrong to attempt matchmaking, although she still believes she was right to dissuade Harriet from marrying Robert Martin.

Emma

The snowy weather gives Emma some respite from confronting Harriet with the news. When it is done, Harriet takes the blow well and does not blame Emma, who is touched to the point of wishing herself more like Harriet. As Austen rather tartly remarks, however, 'it was rather too late in the day to set about being simple-minded and ignorant'.

Emma is left dreading having to confront Mr Elton, but inured as she is to domestic annoyances she realises 'they must encounter each other, and make the most of it.' What will make things more difficult for Harriet? Like Emma, Jane Austen was 'absolutely fixed' in a small circle of acquaintances all her life. There must have been many times when such an intelligent woman was annoyed by or felt critical of members of her circle. Open criticism would not have been appropriate from a woman. It is possible that Austen's ironic point of view was developed as a defence mechanism. Irony would have allowed her to criticise without seeming to be openly hostile. Emma uses the same defence when she visits Miss Bates.

Examination **Coursework**	In any question involving Jane Austen's intentions, it is important to interpret irony correctly. See coursework essay 2, page 60.

Chapter 18

Emma and Mr Knightley discuss Frank Churchill.

Frank Churchill has still not appeared to meet his new stepmother. When Emma and Mr Knightley discuss his absence, we learn a good deal about all

Illusion and delusion

three characters. We glean, first of all, a picture of a wealthy and amiable young man who is at the beck and call of his aunt. While having little time to himself, he is occasionally able to escape to fashionable watering places like Weymouth. Emma is well placed to sympathise with Frank because of her friendship with Mr and Mrs Weston, but also because his situation is not dissimilar from her own. She understands all too well the need for the kind of 'manoeuvring and finessing' that Mr Knightley affects to despise. How are their situations similar?

Austen uses the device of ironic impersonation to reveal Mr Knightley's

Wit and irony

true feelings. The more that Emma praises Frank Churchill, the less Mr Knightley seems to like him and the more unreasonable he becomes. Having spoken reasonably of duty and sacrifice, Mr Knightley goes on to call Frank a 'chattering coxcomb' and a 'puppy', but then contradicts himself by saying he is 'a person I never think of from one month's end to another'. Emma cannot understand Mr Knightley's unreasonable behaviour. It is clear to the reader, however, that it is linked to the warm feelings Emma expresses for Frank.

◼ Self-test questions Chapters 1–18 (Volume 1)

Who? What? Why? When? Where? How?

1　Who marries Mr Weston at the beginning of the novel?
2　What is the reaction of Emma and her father to this marriage?
3　Why does the season at the opening of the novel suit Emma's mood?
4　When did Emma's mother die?
5　Where does Mr Weston live?
6　Who amongst Mr Woodhouse's companions belong to the 'second set' of Highbury society?
7　How does Emma first try to throw Mr Elton and Harriet together?
8　How does Frank Churchill acknowledge his father's marriage?
9　Which characters warn Emma of Mr Elton's real intentions?
10　When does Mr Elton propose to Emma?

Prove it
Provide textual evidence for the following statements.
1　Mr Woodhouse is a valetudinarian.
2　Mr Knightley provides us with a standard against which to judge other characters.
3　Emma has been spoiled by her father and Miss Taylor.
4　Emma has a good deal to put up with.
5　Mr Elton is a social climber.

6   The friendship between Emma and Harriet is not good for either young
    woman.
7   Highbury society is rigidly hierarchical.
8   Isabella is very like her father.
9   Robert Martin is a much more suitable match for Harriet than Emma can
    imagine.
10 Frank Churchill is wrong not to have paid his respects to his father's new wife.

What is the significance?
Identify the speaker, the context of the passage and its significance.
1   'But you must have found it very damp and dirty. I wish you may not catch
    cold.'
2   'I thought him very plain at first, but I do not think him so plain now.'
3   'Her ignorance is hourly flattery.'
4   'The man is almost too gallant to be in love.'
5   'A degradation to illegitimacy and ignorance, to be married to a respectable,
    intelligent gentleman-farmer!'
6   'There is so pointed, and so particular a meaning in this compliment ... that
    I cannot have a moment's doubt as to Mr Elton's intentions.'
7   'I shall often have a niece with me.'
8   'She has no more heart than a stone to people in general; and the devil of a
    temper.'
9   'Everybody has their level, but as for myself, I am not, I think, quite so much
    at a loss.'
10 'If I find him conversible, I shall be glad of his acquaintance; but if he is only
    a chattering coxcomb, he will not occupy much of my time or thoughts.'

Volume 2: Chapter 19

*Emma and Harriet visit Mrs and Miss Bates, who have recently received a letter from
their relation, Jane Fairfax.*

We hear news of Jane Fairfax when Emma and Harriet pay a call on Mrs and

Wit and irony

Miss Bates. What do we learn of this off-stage character? In
the conversation of Miss Bates, Austen provides us with a
comic tour de force. Fractured syntax, unnecessary
circumlocutions and the excessive inclusion of reported speech
with accompanying 'said she's' and 'She often says' all help to
give Miss Bates' speech its flavour. The working of her brain
is revealed as she hops from topic to topic without having the wit to select
only that information which is relevant. How many topics does she cover in
this speech? Miss Bates is no Aunt Sally, however; her simple good nature and
concern for others make her a sympathetic if irritating character, who is often
the target of irony. Having only visited the Bates because she thought she was
safe from one of Jane's letters, Emma can only say, 'I was afraid there could
be little chance of my hearing anything of Miss Fairfax to-day,' when one is
produced.

As well as revealing character, Chapters 18 and 19 serve to give us a picture of life in Highbury. The chief form of entertainment seems to be derived from endless discussion of the doings of friends and acquaintances.

Chapters 20 and 21

Jane Fairfax arrives in Highbury. Harriet is disturbed.

In summarising Jane Fairfax's life-story, Jane Austen reminds us of the wider world outside Highbury, where men fight and die at war and unattached women must earn their living at best as governesses. Given the similarity in their

ages, their intelligence and good looks, one might expect Jane and Emma to become friends, but Emma cannot like her. Mr Knightley thinks 'it was because she saw in her the really accomplished young woman, which she wanted to be thought herself'. Her annoying relative Miss Bates also plays a part in alienating Emma but, when the two meet, Emma is ready to

Emma

be sympathetic towards this sickly looking girl who must soon earn her own living. Jane resists patronage, however, and her superior musical accomplishment and her refusal to be drawn into girlish chat about Frank Churchill cause Emma to judge her 'disgustingly… suspiciously reserved'. Is Emma put off Jane because she cannot patronise her or because she feels belittled?

Examination

A comparison of Jane and Emma might form the basis of a question on character. The girls are similar in age, but very different in character and fortune. Both are intelligent, but Jane is more cultured and better educated. See examination question 2, page 64.

Illusion and delusion

Emma begins to muse on the suspicions that had first begun to form during the visit to Miss Bates: she is convinced that Jane has had an unseemly relationship with Mr Dixon, the bridegroom of her best friend. In dreaming up this fantasy, Emma, the 'imaginist', ignores a much more obvious clue that is staring her in the face. What could it be?

When Mrs Bates and Jane pay a courtesy call at Hartfield they bring news of Mr Elton's engagement to a Miss Hawkins. Emma must now break this news to Harriet. She is assisted in this by the fact that Harriet has just met Robert Martin and his sister in Highbury and feels flustered after the experience. Although Emma is forced to admit to herself that the Martins behaved towards Harriet with 'real feeling' and 'genuine delicacy', while Mr Elton's behaviour has been disappointing, Emma still cannot see that she has done anything very wrong.

Chapters 22 and 23

Harriet visits Abbey-Mill Farm and Frank Churchill arrives in Highbury.

News of Mr Elton's intended bride provides a constant reproach to Emma.

Rank and status

She is able to find some comfort in belittling Augusta Hawkins' relatives and their connections with trade, but Harriet is harder to distract. Emma eventually decides that only a visit to the Martins will suffice to comfort her friend and so she encourages Harriet to accept their invitation to pay a call. Which particular aspect of the visit touches Harriet's heart? When Emma hears details of the visit, she is forced to recognise that she has been a source of pain to Harriet and her friends, but stops short of repentance when she considers their lack of rank. Only a visit to Mrs Weston can help her forget Mr Elton and the Martins.

To provide a contrast with the flatness following the visit to Abbey Farm, Austen uses suspense to build up tension. Emma's disappointment at finding the Westons not at home is assuaged when they stop the carriage to speak to give her some exciting news: Frank Churchill is to come to stay. In his usual over optimistic way, Mr Weston turns the long delay into an advantage – now Frank will be able to stay longer.

By now, the reader is as eager to meet Frank as Emma is, and the excitement created by his arrival is emphasised by the fact that he visits Hartfield much earlier than expected, just as Emma is picturing his arrival at Randalls.

What do Frank's questions about the neighbourhood reveal about his interests? His praise of Mrs Weston endears him to Emma and she is conscious

Illusion and delusion

of how much Mr Weston wants her to like his son. Further evidence of his amiability comes when he announces he must pay a call on Jane Fairfax, whom he had met in Weymouth. His father encourages him to call at once to show Jane she is not thought less of because she is no longer with the wealthy Campbells.

Chapters 24 and 25

Frank Churchill's first days in Highbury.

Frank Churchill's arrival in Highbury triggers an increase in social activity. The

Rank and status

very next day he calls on Emma with Mrs Weston, and Emma shows him around the village. Frank's lively nature is soon made evident when the sight of the ballroom at the Crown prompts him to speculate about the possibility of holding a ball. His rather democratic views on the feasibility of mixing up the ranks is in contrast to Emma's more rigid attitude, but it does not turn her against him. Have you noticed any difference between male and female characters in their attitude to rank? Make a note of these as you read on. What evidence of Frank's good nature has Emma noted so far in this chapter?

Illusion and delusion

Emma finds herself liking Frank more and more as they seem to find common ground in every topic of conversation they touch on. He agrees with her about Miss Bates' talkativeness, he does not seem to find Jane Fairfax attractive and he understands Emma's attitude to Jane's reserved nature. He shares Emma's love of gossip and he provides her with interesting material for her speculations about the nature of the relationship between Jane and Mr Dixon. What is this? Finally, in admiring Mr Elton's Vicarage and making little of its small size he shows that he places the importance of happiness in marriage above wealth. Emma is so charmed by Frank she fails to notice some slight hesitations on Frank's part to discuss Jane Fairfax. At one point there is even a direct attempt to avoid the topic as he hurries into Ford's to buy some gloves. What seems to prompt these avoidance tactics?

Further evidence of Frank's slightly erratic nature is provided on the following day when he travels to London simply to have his hair cut. Mr Knightley is his chief critic when this news gets out.

An invitation from the Coles places Emma in a quandary at this point.

Emma

Previously, Emma has looked down on the family as being 'only moderately genteel' and 'in trade'. When improvements to their home allowed the Coles to begin to entertain their neighbours Emma had hoped for an invitation from them so that she could put them in their place by refusing them. Her feelings are not modified by the fact that she knows that both Mr Knightley and Mr Weston would be happy to socialise with the Coles.

Coursework

The Coles provide useful evidence for a study of attitudes to social position. They are gradually acquiring the trappings of gentility and give us an insight into how social position was calculated by Austen's contemporaries. See coursework essay 2, page 60.

Wit and irony

With great comic effect, Austen traces the about face in Emma's attitude when she realises she is the only person not invited to a dinner which would be attended by Frank Churchill. Her determination to snub the Coles has turned into a feeling of being left out by the time a late invitation arrives. There is heavy irony in the words Austen places in

Emma's mouth as she admits 'she was not absolutely without inclination for the party'. The excuses she gives for accepting an invitation she would once have refused with hauteur are comically inadequate. What are they? The efforts needed to reconcile Mr Woodhouse to the idea of Emma going out remind us of the tedium of Emma's life at home.

Chapter 26

There is a dinner party at the Coles'.

Rank and status

Emma realises that in going to dinner at the Coles' house, she is doing something that had once caused her to feel critical towards Mr Elton. Brighter thoughts replace this rueful reflection when she sees that Mr Knightley has arrived in his carriage. Emma feels that Mr Knightley's habit of walking everywhere is not quite suited to his station in life. The details of the organisation of the party further remind us of the rigid and hierarchical attitude to rank in Highbury. The 'less worthy' females, such as Jane Fairfax and Harriet, are not invited to the meal itself but are to arrive later.

Illusion and delusion

The chief topic of conversation at the dinner table is a piano that has been sent to Jane Fairfax from an anonymous donor. Even the piano is carefully placed in its rank: 'not a grand, but a large-sized square pianoforte'. Emma is now so at ease with Frank Churchill that she shares with him her theory that the piano is a gift from Mr Dixon. Frank provides evidence that seems to confirm this when he tells Emma that Mr Dixon had once saved Jane's life. What is your opinion of Emma's behaviour at this point? Bear in mind that Mr Weston, who sets a standard for considerate behaviour, has observed that Jane is a person who should not be slighted by her betters.

After dinner the other guests arrive. Frank Churchill seems to pay marked attention to Emma but seems to be distracted by Jane Fairfax. Mrs Weston tells Emma that Mr Knightley had sent his carriage to fetch Jane and her aunt to the party. Mrs Weston believes he has done this because he is in love with the niece. Several pieces of evidence are cited by Mrs Weston to support her claim; what are they? She ends by stating her belief that the piano was a present from Mr Knightley to Jane. Emma refuses to believe any of this. The source of her indignation seems to be concern that her nephew might be disinherited

Imagery

by any possible children of Mr Knightley's. Later on, however, she almost begins to believe Mrs Weston when she hears Mr Knightley tell Miss Bates to stop her niece from singing in case she damaged her health. When some impromptu dancing begins, Emma's fears are only allayed when Mr Knightley fails to ask Jane to dance. Her satisfaction is increased when Frank refers slightingly to Jane's dancing. The spontaneity and liveliness of the dancing, the importance placed on the choice of partner and the sorrow expressed when it is over all serve to establish the idea of dancing as an important metaphor for courtship in the novel.

Chapters 27 and 28

Emma and Harriet visit Ford's and the Bateses.

Jane Austen reveals Emma's inner thoughts with ironic wit in order to ensure

Emma

that she maintains the reader's sympathy. We are encouraged to laugh at Emma's arrogance when she thinks about her condescension in visiting the Coles and how they must have admired her. Her concern that she has done wrong in gossiping about Jane with Frank shows she is aware of her faults. Finally, her irritation that Jane should have out-performed her on the piano proves that she is all too human.

Narrative style and structure

In these two chapters, as in so much of the novel, Austen uses a series of visits and the conversation that arises to convey information about character and to move the plot forward. Harriet arrives at Hartfield and tells Emma that she has learned that Robert Martin recently dined with the Coxes, the lawyer's family. Although the daughters of the family are castigated by Emma as being 'very vulgar', Mr Cox, being a lawyer, is of good social standing. Austen is establishing Robert Martin as someone who is accepted in polite society despite Emma's doubts about him. Keep making a note of the qualities that make people acceptable or unacceptable according to Jane Austen. Beware of taking any one character's opinion at face value.

Emma and Harriet go shopping in Ford's where Harriet's dithering over her purchases highlights her general lack of decisiveness. How many times does she change her mind? As Emma looks down the street, we are given a lively sketch of the main street of Highbury. Frank's growing effect on Emma is emphasised by Austen's indication that 'the scene enlarged' on the appearance of Mrs Weston and Frank. They greet Emma on their way to hear Jane's new piano. They are going because Frank has reminded Mrs Weston of a promise she did not remember making. What is the significance of this? At first, Frank seems tempted to join Emma but ends up going with Mrs Weston. Miss Bates soon appears to invite Emma and Harriet to join them – the invitation becomes a long speech in which spectacles, apples, ribbons and Mr Knightley are comically mixed.

At the Bates', we are treated to a scene of domestic intimacy as Frank mends Mrs Bates' spectacles, having already attended to a wobbly piano leg. Jane's

Illusion and
delusion

reticence is in sharp contrast with Frank's conviviality as he plays host to the newcomers. While Jane plays the piano, Frank engages in double talk about Jane's friends in Ireland and speculates about the anonymous donor of the piano. Jane remains calm until she blushes at the mention of dancing in Weymouth. Emma scolds Frank over the pointed nature of his remarks, but he claims not to be ashamed of his meaning. This seems a very harsh remark until we are able to reinterpret this comment later on and realise that he is referring to the early days of his own love for Jane.

Mrs Bates speaks to Mr Knightley through an open window and invites him to join them, but he declines the invitation when he learns that Frank is of the party. This indicates his growing dislike of the young man.

Chapters 29–31

Emma and Frank start making plans for the ball, but they end in disappointment.

There is a steady build-up of excitement as plans for the ball move on apace.

Narrative style
and structure

Lists of guests are compiled, repeated and expanded; rooms are measured and suppers planned, with Frank providing the driving force. After rejecting Randalls as a venue, Frank calls on Emma to discuss the possibility of using the Crown Inn. Mr Woodhouse, typically, does not enter into the spirit of things as he fusses about open windows. You should keep a note of the occasions when his fussing threatens to spoil the enjoyment of others.

Illusion and
delusion

Emma and Frank go to the Crown to make arrangements. Once there, Frank rushes off to seek the opinion of Miss Bates and Jane, of whom he seems to need to be reminded. Mr Weston watches complacently as Frank asks Emma for the first two dances, believing that his own matchmaking is beginning to bear fruit.

The only person not to be caught up in the excitement is Mr Knightley, who seems to be behaving like the valetudinarian Mr Woodhouse. Even Jane Fairfax becomes animated on the topic of the ball. At the height of the excitement, however, Frank is recalled to Enscombe. When Frank comes to take his leave of Emma he lets slip that he has also called at the Bates household and seems about to say something more. Emma believes he is about to declare himself to her, but she gives him no encouragement. The depression she feels in the aftermath of Frank's departure convinces her she must be in love. How does Mr Knightley react to the cancellation of the ball?

Emma's romantic feelings do not last long. When reading Frank's letter fails to move her, she egotistically concludes that he must be more in love than she, and a reference to Harriet in the letter causes her to start planning a new match. Emma needs something to occupy her friend's mind as a date is set for Mr Elton's wedding. She begins to tire of Harriet's moping as the day draws nearer, although her affection is retained by her friend's 'tenderness of heart'.

Chapters 32 and 33

Emma and Harriet visit Mrs Elton, and Mrs Elton visits Hartfield. She reveals her vulgarity, and is particularly patronising to Jane Fairfax.

Mrs Elton is one of Jane Austen's most inspired creations – a character we

Wit and irony

love to hate. There is a slow build-up to the full revelation of Mrs Elton's awfulness. It is a master stroke to introduce Mrs Elton to us when she is in the company of Emma and Harriet. Emma's head is full of the notion that Mr Elton was 'in the same room at once with the woman he had just married, the woman he had wanted to marry, and the woman he had been

expected to marry.' Her first impression is simply that there is 'no elegance' and 'too much ease'. Even so, she has seen enough to realise that Harriet would have made the better wife. Emma is not a completely hopeless matchmaker.

Examination

A careful study of Mrs Elton provides a good deal of material for various examination questions, e.g. use of wit and irony, and attitudes to snobbery. She contributes a good deal to the humour of the novel. See examination essay 1, page 63.

When Mrs Elton returns the visit, her true colours are revealed. Her loquacious and rambling speeches are a less benign version of those of Miss Bates. She condescendingly compares Hartfield to her brother-in-law's 'seat', Maple Grove. She fails to recognise that Hartfield's grounds are not noted for being extensive, thus betraying her lack of experience and taste. Count the

Rank and status

number of times 'Maple Grove' and 'barouche-landau' are repeated. What effect does this have? She drops names that are unknown to Emma and comments impertinently on Mr Woodhouse's health, offering an introduction to Bath society that it is not her place to give. She unblushingly refers to her own musical prowess and attempts to win support from

Emma, who likes to regard herself as queen of Highbury society, to form a musical society. Just when it seems impossible that she could be more blatantly vulgar, she refers to Mrs Weston's previous role as governess and is surprised 'to find her so very ladylike'. Her pretentious and indelicate use of the term 'caro sposo' is a final straw that is hardly needed. 'Caro sposo' is Italian for 'beloved husband': it would not be considered good form for a new bride to boast of her love for her husband. Her vulgar parading of a very little knowledge also sets her a part from characters like Mr Knightley.

A second meeting reveals two even more repugnant aspects of Mrs Elton's character. Her disdainful treatment of Emma and Harriet makes it plain she has heard the full story of the matchmaking and she begins to take up and patronise

Love and marriage

Jane Fairfax. As Mrs Elton proceeds to monopolise Jane, Emma discusses the situation with Mrs Weston and Mr Knightley. When Mr Knightley puts up a warmly expressed defence of Jane's standpoint, Emma hints to him he may be in love. Mr Knightley reveals that Mr Cole had suggested this six weeks previously, but he denies the accusation. What reason does Mr Knightley give for not being attracted to Jane? Emma tactfully turns the conversation to a discussion of another of Mrs Elton's iniquities: her habit of referring to people by their surname alone – another vulgarity.

Chapters 34–36

A dinner is given at Hartfield in honour of Mrs Elton.

These three chapters are all devoted to the dinner held at Hartfield in honour

Narrative style and structure

of the Eltons' marriage. This represents a departure from Austen's usual narrative approach, which is to deal with several events in each chapter. The pace of events slows down and we are given time to dwell on several important revelations that are made in the first of these three chapters.

Illusion and delusion

Seeking to gain Mr Knightley's approval, as ever, Emma invites Jane Fairfax to dine when Harriet declines. John Knightley is also present and begins the conversation by referring to an earlier meeting with Jane when she had been going to the Post Office in the rain. He makes a veiled hint that the letters she was fetching might have been love letters. This is another sign of his perceptive nature – he was the first to hint at Mr Elton's intentions towards Emma. He ends by hoping that one day all her loved ones will all be within her

family circle. This kind thought seems to touch Jane a good deal. She finds it difficult to regain her composure as she is subjected to advice about the weather from all sides, particularly Mrs Elton. Her only defence is to change the topic of conversation. Like all the other women in the novel, apart from Mrs Elton, good manners keep her quiet when she is annoyed.

The discussion of letters gives Emma an opportunity to pronounce Frank Churchill's name. How does Austen give this moment a dramatic build-up? Mr Knightley, never averse to criticising Frank, dismisses his handwriting as being 'like a woman's'. This is, perhaps, his most unforgivable insult and an indication of how his strong feelings are making him lose his judgement. As they walk into dinner, Mrs Elton takes precedence in her usual vulgar way while Emma and Jane enter the dining room arm in arm like friends.

After dinner, Mrs Elton begins to interrogate Jane about finding a place as governess. For once, Jane defends herself assertively, condemning 'the sale – not quite of human flesh – but of human intellect.' Mrs Elton takes this to be a slighting reference to the slave trade and we are led to suspect her brother-in-law was a slave trader, although she specifically denies it. The thick-skinned Mrs Elton continues, unabashed, to dwell on the delights of a situation with one of her friends. What are the attractions of the situations Mrs Elton describes?

Rank and status

Examination

This reference to the slave trade is useful evidence that Jane Austen does not completely ignore events in contemporary society, as some critics imply. Although Austen is mainly concerned with the world in microcosm, she is aware of the bigger picture. See coursework essay 2, page 60.

When Mr Weston arrives late after being away on business, Austen uses the device of interior monologue to convey John Knightley's surprise that a man should be tempted away from his own fireside. Mr Weston brings news that the Churchills are coming to London, which means that Frank will be able to visit more frequently. Austen comments ironically on the way Mr Weston fails to notice that Mr Knightley is not pleased by this news.

Narrative style and structure

In choosing to discuss his son's imminent arrival with Mrs Elton, Mr Weston reveals how completely he is wrapped up in his own concerns. A very funny scene ensues as Mr Weston sings his son's praises and Mrs Elton tries to bring the conversation round to Maple Grove. Neither party wants to listen to the other, but Mrs Elton's determination to be heard is the greater. This type of non-communication occurs several times in the novel. Try to find other examples. Her efforts to dominate the conversation lead Mrs Elton to betray herself in a number of ways. She comically denies that her sister is a fine lady, and in her attempt to prove that her brother-in-law is not *nouveau riche*, she proves once and for all that he is. He has lived in Maple Grove for a mere eleven years – not very long compared with the generations of Woodhouses who have lived at Hartfield.

Wit and irony

The third of the chapters ends with Emma and Mr Knightley arguing amicably over which of them is best placed to look after their nephews. What impression of their relationship is created by their friendly wrangling here? With a final comic touch, the smile is wiped off Mr Knightley's face when he cannot avoid talking to Mrs Elton.

■ Self-test questions Chapters 19–36 (Volume 2)

Who? What? Why? When? Where? How?

1 Who adopted Jane Fairfax?
2 What is Emma's attitude towards Jane?
3 Why does Emma allow Harriet to visit Abbey-Mill Farm?
4 When is the idea of a ball first discussed?
5 Where does Emma first dance with Frank Churchill?
6 How does Mrs Weston shock Emma at the Coles' dinner party?
7 Who mends Mrs Bates' spectacles?
8 What happens to postpone the ball in the Crown?
9 Where do Mrs Elton's sister and brother-in-law live?
10 How does Mrs Elton upset Jane Fairfax when they dine at Hartfield?

Prove it
Provide textual evidence for the following statements.

1 Jane Fairfax has received a better education and has enjoyed a wider experience of the world than Emma.
2 Mr Knightley has an inkling that Mr Elton has proposed to Emma.
3 Frank Churchill has an ulterior motive for visiting Highbury.
4 Mr Knightley and Mr Weston are much more democratic in their social outlook than Emma.
5 Part of Emma's dislike of Jane Fairfax is fuelled by the fact that Jane is more accomplished than she.
6 Mr and Mrs Weston would like Frank to marry Emma.
7 When Jane Fairfax is unwell after the ball is cancelled, Emma believes her 'composure was odious'. In fact, Jane is depressed.
8 Mrs Elton is vulgar.
9 Despite his rather brusque manner, John Knightley has a kindly nature.
10 Despite Mrs Elton's boasting, Mr Suckling, her brother-in-law, has few claims to social status.

What is the significance?
Identify the speaker, the context of the passage and its significance.

1 'Jane was quite longing to go to Ireland, from his account of things.'
2 'Oh! Miss Woodhouse, do talk to me and make me comfortable again.'
3 'I did not know I was to find a pretty young woman in Mrs Weston.'
4 'Did you see her often in Weymouth? Were you often in the same society?'
5 'The sooner every party breaks up the better.'
6 'I must go and ask her if it is an Irish fashion. Shall I?'
7 'Pleasure in seeing dancing! – not I, indeed – I never look at it – I do not know who does.'
8 'That room was the very shape and size of the morning room at Maple Grove.'

9   'He gave me a quiet hint; I told him he was mistaken; he asked my pardon
     and said no more. Cole does not want to be wiser or wittier than his
     neighbours.'
10 'you … who know how very, very seldom I am ever two hours from Hartfield,
     why you should foresee such a series of dissipation for me, I cannot imagine.'

Volume 3: Chapters 37 and 38

The ball at the Crown finally takes place.

Emma contemplates Frank Churchill's return with mixed feelings. She wishes

Illusion and
delusion

to avoid a proposal and hopes that a separation will have
cooled his feelings, and yet she also enjoys the idea of his being
in love with her. When he arrives they meet as friends, but
Frank seems distracted and rushes away to make other calls in
Highbury. Emma believes this 'implied a dread of her
returning power'.

Mrs Churchill's illness takes Frank away again for some
days, until the good news arrives that the Churchills are to settle in nearby
Richmond. With his usual optimism, Mr Weston decides that this will lead
to Frank visiting Highbury more frequently. Now plans for the ball are taken
up again.

On the of the evening of the ball Frank, at first, still seems restless. Emma
is not sure if he is distracted by the arrival of guests or afraid to be near her.
Mrs Elton arrives and approves of Frank in her most patronising manner. She
then adds insult to injury by greeting the newly arrived Miss Bates and Jane
Fairfax as if she were in charge.

Miss Bates is as talkative as ever. Count the number of topics she covers in
her first speech. As soon as she is finished, Mrs Elton begins to monopolise
Jane, fishing for compliments and commenting on Frank Churchill with a little
too much interest.

Rank and status

When the dancing begins there is some confusion over
finding a partner for Mrs Elton, who must be honoured as a
newly married woman. Mr Weston does the honours and, as
Mrs Elton takes precedence again, Emma reflects ironically on
the advantages of marriage.

Irritating though his wife can be, it is left to Mr Elton to
inject real venom into the happy evening. When approached by Mrs Weston
to partner Harriet, he turns her down in a most insolent manner. It is left to
Mr Knightley to come to the rescue and Emma cannot help but admire him
as he dances.

Before supper, Miss Bates returns from seeing her mother to bed and we are treated to a rather touching picture of the old ladies' evening. Luck at cards had been balanced out by the fact that Mr Woodhouse had sent away her favourite dish as being unwholesome. Miss Bates' cheerful chat hides the fact that even a rare evening out is interrupted by family responsibilities, which she seeks to hide from all but Jane.

Examination

An understanding of the character of Miss Bates is important for any question on character, or for a passage-based question.

Emma

Emma has an opportunity to thank Mr Knightley for his kindness to Harriet. Although she will not admit to him the whole reason for the Eltons' enmity towards her, he confides to her that he believes Harriet to be a worthier partner for Mr Elton than his new wife.

Imagery

The evening ends as Emma and Mr Knightley dance together. As Emma says, 'We are not really so much brother and sister as to make it at all improper.' Throughout the ball, the changing of partners in the dance have suggested the comings and goings of courtship. Look back over the chapter and make a note of the couples who have been thrown together or kept apart by the dance.

Examination   Coursework

The ball is an important episode and should be studied carefully. This is when we see the first signs that Emma and Mr Knightley are aware of each other as eligible partners. See examination essay 2, page 64.

Chapters 39 and 40

Emma decides on a new match for Harriet.

The following day, Emma looks back over the evening with satisfaction. Frank had not been over affectionate, she and Mr Knightley had resolved their quarrel over Harriet, and Mr Elton's treatment of Harriet would serve to cure her of her lovesick feelings.

When Frank Churchill arrives bearing a distraught Harriet whom he has rescued from gypsies, Emma cannot resist the temptation to begin matchmaking again. She tells herself that this time she will not interfere, but feels that this will not be necessary.

When Harriet comes to visit a few days later, it is clear she has been cured of her love for Mr Elton and is ready to love another. Even Harriet cannot drop one man for another without due ceremony and so a rather comical ritual takes place as she discards all memories of Mr Elton. Some sticking plaster and the stub of a pencil are discarded. Some days later, she tells Emma that she will never marry, but loves a man who is 'so superior to Mr Elton.' She admires this man because he has done her a great service. Emma takes her to

Illusion and delusion

mean Frank Churchill and the rescue from the gypsies. Because of her resolve not to interfere, Emma does not ask for the name. For the rest of the chapter they speak at cross-purposes about two different men, reminding us of the riddles which Emma had solved so easily but which Harriet found so difficult. Not knowing what she is doing, Emma encourages Harriet to hope. Who else could Harriet be referring to?

Chapter 41

While Emma, Harriet and Mr Knightley are out walking, they bump into the Westons, Frank, Miss Bates and Jane. Emma invites them all back to Hartfield for afternoon tea. Schemes, word games and double dealing ensue.

June arrives and Jane is still at Highbury awaiting the return of the Campbells from Ireland before she takes up a post as governess. Mrs Elton is eager to hurry her off to what is ironically described as 'a delightful situation'.

Illusion and delusion

Mr Knightley has been finding fuel for his dislike of Frank Churchill as he becomes convinced that Frank is trifling with Jane's affections. He observes them at a dinner party and is sure there is an understanding between them. Further evidence comes when Frank seems to have a mysterious prior knowledge of Mr Perry's plans to buy a carriage. In her usual voluble manner, Miss Bates discloses she knew of these plans, and Mr Knightley notices Frank, in some confusion, trying to catch Jane's eye.

This is a scene which does not show Frank in a good light, for his next actions serve to increase Jane's mounting distress. Under the guise of playing a word game, he spells out the word 'blunder' and then, ignoring Emma's cautions, the word 'Dixon'. Mr Knightley, who is concerned for Jane's feelings and distressed at the part that Emma seems to be playing in upsetting her, observes all this. Mr Knightley judges Frank shrewdly, but tends to overreact because of his regard for Emma. He believes Emma to be in some danger:

.she is being tempted to act unworthily and he fears she may have her heart broken by Frank.

It is important to consider Mr Knightley in any question to do with character. He provides a standard by which to measure the behaviour of others.

Examination   Coursework

Illusion and delusion

When Mr Knightley asks Emma about the word game she is embarrassed, but when he goes on to suggest that Frank may be interested in Jane she laughs at his fears. They now continue to converse completely at cross-purposes. Emma thinks Mr Knightley is concerned for Jane because he loves her. Mr Knightley thinks that Emma is certain that Frank loves her, while Emma is equally sure that Frank is in love with Harriet. No wonder, then, that Mr Knightley, who has just begun his dancing career, returns 'to the coolness and solitude of Donwell Abbey'. Like Emma, he seems keen to avoid 'warmer and blinder' emotions. He plays the part of the confirmed bachelor whilst Emma has announced her intention of remaining single. How does Emma usually react to the way Mr Knightley tells her off? What does this reveal about their relationship?

Chapter 42

After a planned trip to Box Hill has to be postponed, an outing strawberry picking at Donwell is decided upon instead.

Mrs Elton attempts to move centre stage in the next two chapters as she organises social gatherings and tries to hurry Jane into a job. An excursion to Box Hill is planned and Mr Weston's over-enthusiastic sociability means that Emma is included in the plans much against her will.

When the trip has to be postponed, Mr Knightley comes to the rescue with the suggestion of a strawberry picking party. Mrs Elton at once appoints herself 'Lady Patroness', saying, 'It is my party. I will bring friends with me', all the while addressing her host as 'Knightley'. She plans the details of her costume aloud, seeming to model herself on Marie Antoinette. How 'natural and simple' are her plans? What type of irony is Austen using here?

Even Mr Woodhouse comes to the party as Mr Knightley has made every effort to make him comfortable. As Emma approaches the Abbey she relishes the scene: a beautiful house and grounds with woodland 'neither fashion nor extravagance had rooted up'. Continuity, reliability and a lack of display are qualities which both Emma and Jane Austen value.

Mrs Elton's speech is described in comic short-hand which begins as an eulogy to strawberries and ends with, 'Could bear it no longer – must

Wit and irony

sit in the shade.' Note the use of dashes for abbreviation and the use of the past tense, which makes this passage a kind of hybrid of reported speech. Once in the shade, Mrs Elton badgers Jane to accept a situation as governess. Meanwhile, Emma observes Mr Knightley and Harriet looking out over a view that includes Abbey-Mill Farm, the home of Robert Martin, but Emma has no fears that Harriet will be prompted to fall in love with Robert again. As Emma gazes at the scene, one thing appears to be out of season. Can you spot it?

Later, Emma comes across Jane Fairfax who announces her intention of

Illusion and delusion

walking home alone. The way she openly shows her feelings of despair at the thought of becoming a governess wins Emma's sympathy. Next, Frank Churchill arrives, very much 'out of humour'. Because of this display of bad temper, Emma is glad she is not in love with him but thinks that Harriet's 'sweet and easy temper will not mind it.' He seems unable to decide whether to eat or not and talks wildly of going abroad,

claiming that he is 'thwarted in everything material'. He prevaricates over coming to Box Hill the following day, but eventually agrees to do so. Emma is still rather proud of the way she is able to influence his actions.

Imagery

The weather plays a part in creating the atmosphere during this episode. It seems in tune with the mood of the characters – hot and uncomfortable. The tempers of Frank and Jane also become heated, and people feel an uncomfortable atmosphere in the party.

Chapter 43

The postponed trip to Box Hill now takes place.

The trip to Box Hill begins well enough, but 'there was a languor, a want of

Love and marriage

spirits, a want of union,' which even Mr Weston cannot dispel. Who is present? Frank Churchill is at first dull and then over-animated, exhibiting the same erratic behaviour that Emma had noted on the previous day. Because she feels let down by the dullness of the day, Emma allows Frank to encourage her into flirtatiousness, while still intending him for Harriet. Frank begins to pretend he can only act on Emma's command and that she,

'who, wherever she is presides,' demands to know what everyone is thinking.

Mrs Elton cannot bear the thought of someone else taking first place and is quick to appoint herself chaperone to the party in order to emphasise her own importance. Mr Knightley questions whether Emma really wants to know what people are thinking.

Wit and irony

Frank's next attempt to liven up the party is to demand that each person should say 'one thing very clever... or two things moderately clever – or three things very dull indeed'. Miss Bates is first to respond. With self-deprecating good humour she speaks of how easy she would find it to say three dull things 'as soon as ever I open my mouth.' Emma's response may not seem very shocking at first, 'Pardon me – but you will be limited as to number – only three at once', but it is more than a trivial example of bad manners. Once again, Emma has been tempted to use irony to protect herself from the tedium of everyday life at Highbury.

Examination   Coursework

The outing to Box Hill is an important episode and should be studied carefully. Emma's rudeness to Miss Bates creates a high spot of tension in a novel that covers domestic, small-scale events.

Although Miss Bates does not have the intellect 'to frighten those who might hate her' into submission, her simple good nature wins her the affection

Rank and status

of all the well-intentioned characters in the novel. We have seen that it is considered important, in Highbury, to treat those with little money with extra consideration. Like the author, Miss Bates is the impecunious daughter of a clergyman. Jane Austen would have understood, at a personal level, how important decorum and consideration for others were in preserving the self-respect of the disadvantaged. In a time of swiftly changing fortunes, it is important for a society to acknowledge that wealth alone cannot buy respect. Decorum is the social glue that holds a society together. Emma's outburst, therefore, is not just extremely cruel, it is anti-social and is calculated to shock us in the way that racist behaviour would shock us today.

Mr Weston comes to the rescue and glosses over an awkward moment with a conundrum which, if it had been posed by anyone else, would have been

Love and marriage

intended ironically. Why is this so? Mr and Mrs Elton leave to go for a walk and Frank comments disparagingly on the way they met in a public place with no previous connection. Jane Fairfax points out that those who form hasty attachments always have an opportunity to end them. Frank reacts by asking Emma to find him a wife with hazel eyes – the very colour of Harriet's.

When Jane and her aunt and Mr Knightley move away, Frank becomes even more excitable. Emma grows weary of him and is glad when they make a move to return home.

Mr Knightley makes an opportunity to speak to Emma about her behaviour. He points out to her that Miss Bates' poverty demands their sympathy and that Emma's position means that other people might copy her disrespectful attitude. Once more, they find themselves at cross-purposes. Mr Knightley interprets her silence as a stubborn refusal to listen to advice. When Emma tries to make amends he has gone. Emma 'never had been so depressed.' The journey home sees her in tears.

Examination   Coursework

Charlotte Brontë accused Jane Austen of ignoring human passions. Evidence of strong feelings is useful when discussing characterisation. Much of the tension of the novel is created by the gradual revelation that Emma and Mr Knightley are in love.

Chapter 44 and 45

Emma tries to make amends for her behaviour at Box Hill.

The very next day, Emma makes a penitential call on Miss Bates, rather hoping that Mr Knightley will notice and approve her action. There is quite a bustle before she is admitted to the room. In her usual discursive fashion Miss Bates lets slip the information that Jane is very upset and disturbed, but would probably have stayed in the room had the visitor been Mrs Cole. We are told that Jane has written to accept a situation with Mrs

Emma

Elton's friend, the one she had turned down so strenuously at Donwell. We are left to decide for ourselves why she could not face Emma. Is it the contrast in their fortunes that upsets Jane, or does she still resent the insult which Miss Bates apparently forgives so readily?

Illusion and delusion

As Miss Bates rambles on it becomes clear that Jane made her decision to accept the post at the very time they heard that Frank Churchill left suddenly for Richmond. The incidental information we are given about John Abdy needing parish relief foreshadows the fate that could await the three portionless women of the Bates household. Mention of the piano forces Emma to remember with guilt the scurrilous jokes she had

**Love and
marriage**

shared with Frank concerning the donor of the gift. Now she can feel nothing but sympathy for Jane.

When Emma returns home, Harriet and Mr Knightley are there. He is so pleased to hear Emma has been to visit Miss Bates that he takes her hand and almost kisses it, although he decides not to at the last moment. This might seem a small gesture to us, but the moment is charged with emotion. 'Emma's colour was heightened'; Mr Knightley looks at her 'with a glow of regard', and Emma is 'warmly gratified'. Notice the vocabulary suggestive of heat that is used at this point. Customs may change, but there is no mistaking the language of strong emotions.

Examination   **Coursework**

Use this episode as evidence when discussing Jane Austen's portrayal of strong emotions. This incident provides us with further evidence of the growing regard that Emma and Mr Knightley feel for each other. See coursework essay 1, page 59.

The following day, news is heard which makes Emma forget Jane's troubles for a while: Mrs Churchill is dead. Even Mr Weston, who had suffered so

Emma

much at her hands, makes an attempt to mourn her, but soon all thoughts turn to Frank's prospects. Emma is pleased to think he will now be at liberty to marry Harriet.

Emma now tries very hard to show support for Jane. How does she do this? All offers are turned down and Emma is rather mortified to hear that Mrs Elton, Mrs Cole and Mrs Cox have been admitted into Jane's presence while she has been denied. Her comfort is the knowledge that she has now treated Jane with consideration and that Mr Knightley will be pleased with her.

Chapters 46 and 47

The secret liaison between Frank Churchill and Jane Fairfax is finally revealed. Emma does not look forward to breaking the news to Harriet, but is surprised by her reaction.

Ten days after Mrs Churchill's death, Emma receives a mysterious summons from Mrs Weston. It is obvious to Emma that Mr Weston believes they have bad news for her, but she is kept in suspense until she can speak to Mrs Weston.

The news is that Frank and Jane Fairfax have been secretly engaged since the previous October, when they were both staying at Weymouth. Emma can think of only two things: the foolish things she has said to Frank

Love and marriage

concerning Jane and Mr Dixon, and the match she had hoped to make between Frank and Harriet. Mrs Weston's fear is that Emma had been in love with Frank and that she had hoped to marry him. Mrs Weston is soon reassured, but Emma cannot be comforted so easily. Here mind goes back over the previous months and she finds much to blame in Frank's behaviour. She realises that Jane has had a good deal to endure, as she has been forced to watch her fiancé flirting with another woman. She wonders why Frank let Jane go ahead with her plans to get a job and is told that Frank did not know. She is told that Mr Churchill has agreed to the marriage that would have been condemned by the aunt. There is a moment of dramatic irony as Mrs Weston says, 'I have always had a thoroughly good opinion of Miss Fairfax. I never could, under any blunder have spoken ill of her,' and we realise that Emma has said many things she is now sorry for.

Emma

Once more, Emma is left with the responsibility of comforting Harriet while knowing that she is to blame for her friend's predicament. This time, her feelings are even more complicated. She is glad to be able to feel angry with Frank as well as herself. It dawns on her that Jane has turned down all her proffered kindnesses because of the flirtation that had seemed to be going on between her and Frank.

Having dreaded the confrontation with Harriet, Emma is astonished to find that Harriet already knows the news and does not seem to mind at all. It takes

Imagery

her some time to convince Emma that she is not in love with Frank Churchill. In the end she has to name the true object of her affections: it is Mr Knightley. The service rendered which had won her heart was not being rescued from the gypsies, but being asked to dance after Mr Elton had refused her. When Harriet tells Emma that she believes that Mr Knightley returns her affection, Emma realises 'with the speed of an arrow, that Mr Knightley must marry no one but herself!' What are Harriet's proofs that Mr Knightley loves her?

Examination

This rare use of imagery serves to underline the heightened emotion of this episode, and should be mentioned in any discussion of Jane Austen's style. See coursework essay 1, page 59.

Emma begins to be convinced by Harriet's reasoning. When she is alone and thinks back over the previous year, she realises she had never loved Frank but had always been in love with Mr Knightley. The most bitter irony she has to endure is that she was the person who had encouraged Harriet to look for a more worthy husband than Robert Martin.

Chapters 48 and 49

Emma reflects on recent events, and the revelation that she has been so wrong about so many people's feelings and motives. Mr Knightley comes to comfort Emma, and both are surprised by further revelations.

Emma spends a good deal of time thinking about Mr Knightley. She realises

Emma

she has always wanted to be first in his affections. She concludes that if Harriet has proof of his affection, she knows that Mr Knightley is aware of all her faults. She hopes that Mr Knightley will remain single and comes to the rather odd conclusion that she would not marry him herself if he asked her! What does this decision reveal about her state of mind?

Mrs Weston breaks in on her thoughts with news of Jane Fairfax, who has confided in her about the pain caused by the secret engagement. Emma can now understand what it is like to be in love and finds it easier to sympathise with Jane, especially as Jane sends a message of thanks to Emma for the concern shown during Jane's illness. Emma finds it difficult to listen as her mind is on Mr Knightley.

When Mrs Weston is gone, Emma wishes she had listened to Mr Knightley

Imagery

and made more of a friend of Jane as this would have prevented her from interfering in Harriet's relationship with Robert Martin. The weather is cold and autumnal although it is only July. She thinks of the future and imagines she will see less of Mrs Weston once her child is born. Austen creates a mood of gloom to provide a contrast with the scene which

follows. Emma is back where she started, in the gloomy mood she was feeling at the beginning of the novel.

Later that afternoon, the weather clears and Emma's mood lightens as she walks in the shrubbery. It is here that Mr Knightley finds her. He believes that she is upset over the engagement of Frank Churchill and has come to comfort her. For the last time they are at cross-purposes. Emma explains that she is not upset but he believes, at first, that she is putting on a brave face.

Illusion and delusion

When at last he accepts that she is telling the truth, he wishes that he was as lucky as Frank. Emma now believes him to be referring to his wish to marry Harriet and prevents him from saying more. Realising that she has hurt him by cutting him short, Emma asks him to continue. At last all misunderstandings are cleared up and Mr Knightley asks Emma to marry him. Note the strength of the verbs and adjectives used in Mr Knightley's proposal speech to convey strong emotion. Emma has time to feel sorry for Harriet but, with an unsentimental practicality, accepts Mr Knightley's offer, although Jane Austen is far too discreet to tell us what she said.

We are now given an insight into the development of Mr Knightley's love for Emma. He had begun to realise he loved her at the same time he had started to dislike Frank Churchill, and had eventually realised that his dislike of Frank was based on jealousy. After the trip to Box Hill, when Emma had seemed to flirt so openly with Frank, Mr Knightley had decided to go away. He had only returned in order to comfort Emma and had been overjoyed to discover she did not need it.

Chapters 50 and 51

Emma makes plans for her father and for Harriet. A letter arrives from Frank Churchill that clears up more mysteries.

Although happy that Mr Knightley has proposed to her, Emma is left with two worries: her father and Harriet. She decides she cannot marry while she has her father to look after and that Harriet must be sent to London to stay with the John Knightleys in Brunswick Square.

A letter arrives from Frank Churchill that clears up many mysteries. Frank

is careful to accept all the blame for the secret engagement and does not appear in a very good light. He points out that he only came to Highbury once Jane was there and has only charming words to make up for the slight to Mrs Weston. He claims that he never felt that Emma was in danger of falling in love with him. He explains that his flirtatious manner towards Emma was calculated to hide his true feelings for Jane.

He confesses that he almost told Emma the truth and felt, in any case, that she had probably guessed it. The piano was a gift from him. On the day Jane had left the strawberry party early, he had met her on the road and quarrelled with her. They had quarrelled again after the trip to Box Hill because of his flirtatious behaviour with Emma. Jane had told him of her intention to take up the post with Mrs Smallridge, but he forgot to post the letter that was meant to prevent her from doing so.

It is, perhaps, a long and rather tedious letter for the modern reader to wade through at this interesting point in the novel. It is, however, a useful narrative device that clears up many mysteries. It is worth noting that many novels of the period made great use of letters and the contemporary reader would be used to this. Much of the information given in the letter is repeated later to ensure that even the least alert reader understands the twists and turns of the plot.

Emma is ready to forgive Frank once she has read the letter. Mr Knightley softens his opinion of Frank but still believes him 'to be happier than he deserves.' Finally, the question of marriage is settled. Emma's decision to defer marriage while her father lives is overturned when Mr Knightley suggests he should move to live at Hartfield. It only remains to break the news to Mr Woodhouse. Now Emma could be happy if it were not for poor Harriet.

  This letter is useful for detecting earlier clues to Frank's secret engagement, and should be discussed in any question concerning narrative style.

Examination   Coursework

Chapters 52 and 53

Harriet leaves to visit Isabella and her family in London. Emma visits Jane Fairfax, and the news of Emma's engagement is finally broken to Mr Woodhouse.

Although Harriet has never spoken a word of resentment to Emma over her

Emma

engagement to Mr Knightley, Emma is glad to see her go to London. She puts off her other problem – the matter of announcing her marriage to her father – until after the birth of Mrs Weston's child.

Having put her concerns to one side, Emma decides to visit Jane. The visit has an attraction for her because she and Jane are in the same position as engaged women. She is not sure how she will be received and is glad to receive a warm welcome. Mrs Elton is also there and seems to be relishing being in on a secret, which she believes to be known only to her. Jane's situation is alluded to with many half-veiled references that become almost unbearable. She seems to taunt Emma with superior knowledge when she comments about Mr Perry's skill in curing Jane, while in fact Emma knows Jane has been lovesick rather than unwell. Comically, Miss Bates, who is usually so verbose is, by comparison, the soul of discretion.

Illusion and delusion

Emma has the satisfaction of proving that she knows more about some matters than Mrs Elton when she is able to correct her on the time of a meeting between Mr Elton and Mr Knightley. Furthermore, when Mr Elton arrives she has the pleasure of hearing that Mr Knightley has become very difficult to find these days. She, of course, knows that it is because he has been paying court to her.

When Emma takes her leave of Jane, the two women speak openly of Jane's forthcoming marriage and seek each other's forgiveness for previous misunderstandings. As Emma departs with the words, 'Oh! If you knew how much I love everything that is decided and open!', we realise that she has finally learned that it is not as easy as she had once thought to read and manipulate situations.

However, Emma still has two areas of secrecy in her own life. She feels she cannot discuss Harriet with Mr Knightley but, as soon as Mrs Weston is

Emma

available to lend her support, she is at least able to break the news of her impending marriage to her father. Much persuasion is needed from Isabella, as well as Mrs Weston, but Mr Woodhouse is eventually reconciled. If Emma has been guilty of errors of judgement in the course of the novel, the difficulties she experiences in dealing with her father ensure she usually has our sympathy. Inevitably, once Mr Weston knows the news, he spreads it all around Highbury. The Eltons' reception of the news is predictably sour and Mrs Elton dwells on two particular reasons for disliking to hear it. What are they?

Chapters 54 and 55

All remaining misunderstandings are resolved, and a happy future seems assured for all concerned.

Emma begins to dread Harriet's return from London as the one problem left in her life. One day, however, Mr Knightley breaks news that he believes will be unwelcome to her, but which actually comes as a relief. Harriet is to marry Robert Martin. Emma finds it difficult to believe that Harriet could have so quickly forgotten Mr Knightley. Mr Knightley believes that Emma finds it difficult to accept that the match has been made because of her disapproval

Illusion and delusion

of Robert Martin. Emma is able to reassure her fiancé that she is now prepared to accept Robert Martin, while Mr Knightley admits that he has changed his mind about Harriet, having taken the trouble to talk to her in order to know her better. At last, Emma understands the reason for the interest Mr Knightley had taken in Harriet.

The Westons arrive with Jane and Frank, and some final misunderstandings and mysteries are cleared up. Emma assures Frank she did not guess his secret, and he admits that he once came near to confessing to her – she realises that this was the time when she thought he was going to propose. Frank proves how incorrigible he is when he is still tempted to laugh over the Mr Dixon affair, but generously takes the blame for it. Finally, the mystery of his knowing about Mr Perry's carriage is cleared up. What is Jane's reaction to his mentioning this? Emma still instinctively likes Frank, but finds on this occasion that her sympathies lie with Jane. Emma is capable of learning from experience while Frank is simply happy to have got away with his scrape.

When Harriet returns from London, there is some embarrassment between the two friends which soon clears up when Harriet admits she has been self-deceived. Emma now realises that Harriet had always liked Robert and has been finally won over by his willingness to wait for her.

Love and marriage

Wit and irony

Harriet and Robert are married in September, while Jane and Frank are to be married in November. A series of robberies encourages Mr Woodhouse to agree to an October wedding for Emma. He feels that Mr Knightley will protect the house. The final note of irony is supplied by Mrs Elton: 'Very little white satin, very few lace veils; a most pitiful business!' By this we are to understand that the ceremony has been conducted with the kind of understated good taste that Mrs Elton, with her lace and her pearls, will never be able to understand.

■ Self-test questions Chapters 37–55 (Volume 3)

Who? What? Why? When? Where? How?
1 Who moved from Yorkshire, to London and then to Richmond?
2 What did Emma think of Mr Weston when she arrived early at the ball?
3 Why did Mr Knightley dance with Harriet at the ball?
4 When did Mr Knightley hold a strawberry picking party?
5 How did Emma upset Miss Bates at Box Hill?
6 Who offers Jane a post as governess, which she accepts?
7 What surprising news is broken to Emma by Mrs Weston ten days after Mrs Churchill's death?
8 Why does Harriet go to London?
9 How does Harriet get over her love for Mr Knightley?
10 What finally persuades Mr Woodhouse to agree to Emma's wedding?

Prove it
Provide textual evidence for the following statements.
1 By the end of the ball, Emma's attachment to Mr Knightley is clear.
2 When Jane is ill, she would have accepted a visit from Mrs Cole although she refuses one from Emma.
3 Jane Fairfax decides to accept Mrs Smallridge's offer of a post as governess only after hearing that Frank has returned to Richmond.

4   Mr Woodhouse shows a lack of sympathy when he hears that Jane is to be a governess.
5   Once Emma realises she loves Mr Knightley, she still does not completely understand her real feelings.
6   Mr Knightley believes that Emma is heartbroken over news of Frank and Jane's engagement.
7   Emma was already unknowingly in love with Mr Knightley when Mrs Weston suggested he was in love with Jane Fairfax.
8   Mr Weston is an incorrigible gossip.
9   Frank never feels as much shame as Emma does about the way he treated Jane.
10 By the end of the novel, Harriet has achieved a measure of self-knowledge.

What is the significance?
Identify the speaker, the context of the passage and its significance.
1   'I have a great curiosity to see Mrs Elton, I have heard so much of her. It cannot be long, I think, before she comes.'
2   'I would get you a better partner than myself. I am no dancer.'
3   'The service he rendered you was enough to warm your heart.'
4   'Blunder.'
5   'The thing would be for us all to come on donkeys, Jane, Miss Bates, and me – and my caro sposo walking by.'
6   'Miss Fairfax's compliments and thanks, but is quite unequal to any exercise.'
7   'What could he mean by such a horrible indelicacy? To suffer her to engage herself – to suffer her to even think of such a measure!'
8   'You do not think I care about Mr Frank Churchill?'
9   'If I loved you less, I might be able to talk about it more.'
10 'Very little white satin, very few lace veils; a most pitiful business!'

How to write a coursework essay

Different examining boards have different requirements for A Level coursework, but there are certain principles that hold good in every case. We will consider these and also two possible titles for coursework. However, essays can be not only of *different lengths*, but of *different types*. You are probably most likely to find yourself writing on one text (approximately 1,500–2,000 words), comparing two texts (3,000 words) or writing about a literary genre referring to at least three texts (up to 5,000 words). Most of these word-length requirements are optional maximums; *it is essential that you check with your teacher that there is no penalty for extra length.*

If you are choosing a *comparative* title, you must make sure that comparisons are made throughout, not necessarily in the same sentence, but at least in adjacent paragraphs. Your essay title must direct you to some specific comparison, not just a generalised survey of similarities and differences. Remember also that 'comparison' always implies 'contrast' as well – discussing different ways of approaching a theme, plot-line or genre can always be productive.

The single-text coursework essay is in many ways similar. A specific task is again essential, and once again your theme or line of argument must be kept before the reader throughout. Narration is almost always unhelpful: even at A level, 'telling the story' is the most common failing. Almost equally dangerous is taking opinions from critics without fully understanding them and failing to absorb them into your arguments. *Copying* from critics without acknowledgement is, of course, plagiarism and can result in disqualification.

The need for a developing argument or comparison has implications for your method of approaching the essay. You should make general notes on the material (textual evidence, useful quotations, comments by critics, etc), then shape them into an ordered framework (probably simply by numbering them in an appropriate order) before working through at least two or three drafts of the essay. You should be fully aware of what each paragraph is to be about, as far as possible signalling this to the reader in the first sentence, often called the *topic sentence* for this reason. With comparatively short essays like these, you should make sure that your style is concise and time is not wasted on unnecessary quotations. Relevant, fairly brief quotations are very valuable, absorbed into your sentences if very short, or set out on separate lines if slightly longer. It is unlikely that quotations of more than a few lines will really help you.

The actual presentation of your essay is also important. With coursework it is sheer carelessness to make errors in spelling, punctuation or syntax or (worst of all) to confuse or misspell characters' names. Unless there is a definite reason for doing so, avoid slang and colloquialisms, including contractions like 'they've' for 'they have'.

The format of introduction-essay-conclusion is perfectly acceptable, but, used over-formally, can weight the essay too much in the direction of semi-relevant generalisation at the beginning and the end. In a good essay, the conclusion will simply be the final stage of a developed argument.

Each of the example titles given below can be easily adapted to a comparative essay with another text(s). Use the outlines to form your notes on this text. The points should also help you to focus your approach to the other text(s).

An *outline* of a model answer has been supplied for each essay title below. Use this outline in conjunction with material in the **Who's who**, **Themes, images and language** and **Text commentary** sections of this guide. In addition, the points raised as **Examiner's tips** throughout the Text commentary should prove particularly useful.

1 *What has Jane Austen to say about courtship and marriage in* Emma *and how does she convey her opinions on this topic?*

An obvious way to gather material for this essay is to look at all the couples in the novel. We are given a wide range of information about many relationships at different stages of development. Each couple throws light on a different aspect of love and courtship.

If we look at the experiences of the courting couples, we see that courtship is generally portrayed as a time of difficulty and emotional turmoil leading to happy resolution at the time of marriage.

Austen uses the recurring motifs of dance and the posing of riddles or word games to highlight the communication difficulties inherent in courtship. This theme is also illuminated by the number of conversations that are held at cross-purposes.

Modern readers may be misled by the lack of reference to passionate feelings. Careful examination of the text will reveal that most of the couples feel strongly about each other. When Emma dances with Mr Knightley a good deal of sexual tension is hinted at. Diction is used in several passages to indicate heightened emotion. The pathetic fallacy is also used as a sign of strong emotions.

Some of the difficulties of courtship arise from the difficulties involved in finding the right partner. The Churchills provide us with an example of a marriage made difficult by the domineering attitude of one partner. Jane Fairfax compares her own engagement to that of the Eltons when she worries that her secret engagement was over-hasty. Harriet Smith is the archetype of the young woman who cannot make up her mind. Just in case the reader is tempted to become over-serious about the difficulties of marriage, those who fear commitment are satirised by Mr Woodhouse with his, 'Poor Miss Taylor!' He views marriage as a kind of death.

For the women characters, apart from Emma who is independently wealthy, marriage is seen as a financial necessity. The Bates family, including Jane Fairfax, illustrate the fate that awaits unattached women of no means.

Marriage is also seen as a source of personal fulfilment for both parties. The Eltons are the only partners who have married purely for material gain and they are portrayed unsympathetically. Even Mrs Churchill is mourned by her husband.

2 *Would you agree with a contemporary of Jane Austen who described this novel as 'nothing more than a harmless amusement'? Discuss Austen's possible intentions in writing this novel.*

Jane Austen's light and witty tone misleads some readers who imagine she has no serious intention. The fact that she confines her plot to 'Three or four families in a country setting' and works on a 'little bit (two inches wide) of ivory' adds to the misapprehension that Austen avoids serious themes.

Although the setting is rural, events in the wider world are touched upon. Little is made of the fact that Jane Fairfax's father dies in battle and the suspicion that Mrs Elton's father was a slave trader, but the whole novel hinges on the new social mobility that allows Mr Weston to build Randalls and Mr Cole to buy a carriage. We see the different possible responses to this social change as Emma comes to terms with Harriet's marriage to Robert Martin. Jane's protestation against the governess trade is expressed as passionately as anything written by Charlotte or Emily Brontë.

Although the main theme of the novel is courtship and marriage, the subject is not treated lightly or romantically. The practical advantages of marriage for women such as Jane or Harriet are dealt with unsentimentally. The author mainly deals with the difficulties rather than the joys of courtship.

Austen is also interested in other aspects of human relationships. Although the scale is small, there are examples of cruelty in the novel. Mr Elton's refusal to dance with Harriet and Emma's cruel remark to Miss Bates are both fuelled by snobbery. The democratic kindness of Mr Knightley and other characters is a plea for tolerance and harmony that is reflected in the description of the landscape around Donwell Abbey.

How to write an examination essay

Preparation

- The *first essential* is thorough revision. You may be answering questions in either a traditional examination or an Open Book examination. It is vital that you remember that in an Open Book examination you have enough time to look up quotations and references, but *only if you know where to look*.

- The revision process should begin well before the examination: a matter of months rather than weeks. Initially you need to re-read texts, which is not a good idea the week before the examination. It is then useful to make notes, both to assist memory at the time and to provide a summary for later revision. These notes should be arranged to give a pattern to your study: by themes, characters, techniques, etc. Quotations should not be learned simply by rote, but together with relevant uses for them. A late stage of revision should be to fix the patterns of knowledge in your mind, probably by writing practice essays.

- The time process is very important – trying to absorb new material the night before the examination is likely to be positively harmful.

Before you start writing

- Read the questions very carefully, both to choose the most suitable title and to be certain of exactly what you are asked to do. It is very easy, but potentially disastrous, to answer the essay you *hope or imagine* has been asked, or to reproduce a practice essay you wrote on a vaguely similar theme.

- A Level questions need careful attention. Do not respond instantly to a quotation without checking what the question asks you to write about it. Make certain that you are aware of every part of a question: many ask you to do two or three distinct things, and omitting one of these immediately reduces your possible marks. Check for words like compare, contrast, analyse, consider and discuss.

- You do not have much spare time in an examination, but it is worthwhile spending a few minutes noting down the material you think is relevant, matching it with the instructions you have been given and drawing up an essay plan. Starting on the wrong essay or starting the right one in the wrong way ultimately wastes time.

- Make sure that your plan develops a consistent argument or point of view – you will not be asked to tell the story, and essays that take a chronological approach seldom do well.

Writing the essay

- The first sentences are very important. You should begin the essay by informing the examiner of the opinion you are going to develop, the contrasts you are going to study or your view of the problem you are about to analyse. This should stay in focus throughout the essay – if possible, each paragraph should begin with a topic sentence relating the material of that paragraph to your overall theme or argument.

- Do not spend too long introducing the essay: move quickly to the material you wish to cover. Throughout, check your plan to make sure that you deal with all the points you wish to make.

- Quotation is particularly relevant where the style of expression is important in itself or in revealing character or the author's viewpoint. It is less important when you are referring to events. Quotations should be kept fairly short and should be relevant, not simply attractive or well known. In many cases it is possible to absorb a quotation into your sentence, but quotations of a few lines must be set out separately and as in the text.

- There is no 'correct' length for an essay. The fact that someone else is clearly writing huge amounts does not mean that he or she will obtain better marks than you. However, you should make sure that you use your time fully, write concisely and avoid padding.

- It is dangerous to exceed the allotted time for each question by more than a few minutes, especially as marks can always be gained most easily at the start of an essay. Make sure that you tackle the required number of questions. For this reason, though an elegant conclusion is desirable, it may sometimes be necessary to omit it.

- Examiners understand that candidates are writing under pressure, but it is still important that you maintain as high a standard of written expression as possible. Avoid slang, colloquialisms and contractions (e.g. 'they've' for 'they have') wherever possible.

Examination questions inevitably invite the candidate to present an argument. Decide on your position and make sure that you refer to both sides of the argument. Whether the question pertains to a theme or a specific scene in the text, you must demonstrate your knowledge of the whole text. Make sure that you refer to specific examples throughout the novel in your argument.

An *outline* of a model answer has been supplied for each essay title below. Use this outline in conjunction with material in the **Who's who, Themes, images and language** and **Text commentary** sections of this guide. In addition, the points raised as Examiner's tips throughout the Text commentary should prove particularly useful.

1 *Look again at the second half of Chapter XV (15), Mr Elton's proposal to Emma (from 'Isabella stepped in after her father,' to the end of the chapter). Comment on both the purpose and the effect of the comedy in this scene and in* **two other** *episodes of your choice from* Emma.

In tackling this type of question, beware of the following pitfalls:

- The question may well focus attention on a particular aspect of the passage, but do not be tempted to comment on irrelevant points.

- You are always required to show knowledge of other parts of the text. Although the examiner will not expect you to divide your attention between the two halves of the question exactly, it can be difficult to produce a coherent and well-structured answer to this type of question.

In answering this question, you need to comment on:

- the purpose of this scene;
- the comic elements of the scene;
- two comparable scenes from *Emma*.

The main purpose of this scene is to reveal Emma's delusions about Mr Elton. Up until this point she has been very confident in her role as a matchmaker, despite warnings from the Knightley brothers. Although we have had ironic hints from Austen that Emma is not all that she seems, this is the first, but not the last, time that we see Emma openly revealed as having been wrong.

Another purpose is to show Mr Elton in his true colours. We have previously seen him through Emma's eyes as a suitable partner for Harriet. Now he is revealed as a calculating social climber. As the novel proceeds, our opinion of him will deteriorate further. We can no longer accept Emma as a reliable witness and will become even more sceptical of her ability to judge others as the novel progresses.

The comic tone of this scene contrasts with the quieter, more subdued tone of the following chapter as Emma contemplates having to tell Harriet about the proposal. Much of the humour of this passage comes from dramatic irony. Emma has expected a very different outcome to all her efforts to throw Mr Elton and Harriet together. Now she realises that Mr Elton has interpreted her machinations as encouragement. Further humour is derived from the fact that Emma and Mr Elton talk at cross-purposes for a while as she struggles to believe that Mr Elton is proposing to Harriet by proxy.

Another source of humour is the swiftly changing emotions of the protagonists. Emma moves from vague apprehension to shock and devastation. Her attempt to restrain her companion with talk of the weather satirises English reserve. Mr Elton moves from over-confident ardour to sulky silence. The stiff formality of their farewells is in comic contrast to the heightened emotions of the proposal and refusal.

Another passage that satirises snobbery comes in Chapter 36, when Mrs Elton and Mr Weston attempt to hold a conversation. The link with Mr Elton makes this a good choice of passage to discuss. There is also a certain amount of talking at cross-purposes as Mrs Elton attempts to extol the glories of Maple Grove while Mr Weston tries to sing the praises of his son.

A second passage to discuss might be another scene of disillusionment, this time for Harriet, as she gives up the relics of her love for Mr Elton, which she had once treasured. Here the tone of the humour is gentle. While we smile at Harriet's naïveté, we do not condemn her as we do Mr Elton. Again, Harriet and Emma talk at cross-purposes as Harriet talks of her new love. In all three passages, the difficulties of real communication are highlighted.

2 'We end by liking Emma.' How far do you agree with this statement and what relevance do you think it has to Jane Austen's purpose?

This is another popular format for examination questions. The danger for candidates lies in failing to notice the second half of the question. The first half of the question is asking for your opinion of Emma. The second half is asking you about Austen's intention in manipulating the reader's response to the main character.

Your opinion of Emma is going to be a matter of personal taste. Some readers find it difficult to overcome their disapproval of Emma's initial snobbery and bossiness. It is important, however, to give due consideration to the evidence provided in the text. Emma always shows genuine contrition when she has hurt someone, whether it is Harriet, Jane Fairfax or Miss Bates. She is slow to learn from her mistakes, but this is a very human failing. Emma can be impetuous and often tramples on the feelings of others, but she is shown to have a greater sense of decorum than Frank Churchill. She learns the error of judging others by snobbish standards and is certainly not in the same league as Mrs Elton as far as this fault is concerned. Finally, we have to accept that she earns the approval of the worthiest character in the novel or he would not have asked her to marry him.

The quotation points us towards one of Austen's purposes in writing the novel. She deliberately manipulates our view of Emma so that we are forced to reassess our opinion of her as the novel progresses. One of the themes of the novel is illusion and delusion. We are shown that Emma finds it difficult to judge others. By forcing us to change our minds about Emma, Austen also shows us that we, the readers, find it difficult to assess Emma. Because we see most events from Emma's point of view, we go through the learning process with her.

Self-test answers Chapters 1–18 (Volume 1)

Who? What? Why? When? Where? How?

1 Miss Taylor.
2 Both are unhappy, but Emma tries to take a positive view in order to cheer up her father.
3 The season is autumn – the end of summer and, therefore, a sad season in keeping with Emma's mood.
4 Too long ago for Emma to remember her clearly.
5 At Randalls, which he had built for himself.
6 Mrs Bates, Miss Bates and Mrs Goddard.
7 By painting Harriet's portrait.
8 By writing him a letter. He claims that the demands of Mrs Churchill make it impossible to visit in person.
9 First Mr Knightley warns her that Mr Elton will want to marry money, then John Knightley tells her that he thinks Mr Elton is taking an interest in her.
10 At Christmas, on the way home from dinner at Randalls.

Prove it

1 He hates change, especially when it comes in the form of marriage. He worries about his health and is fussy about food. He is fearful of bad weather and catching colds.
2 When we first meet him, Mr Knightley shows sense in ignoring Mr Woodhouse's fuss over the weather. He encourages Emma and her father to see the good side to Miss Taylor's marriage. He sees the danger in Emma's friendship with Harriet and is the first to warn Emma that Mr Elton will not marry her friend; he also detects the relationship between Jane and Frank. He reprimands Emma for her treatment of Miss Bates. Even his dislike of Frank Churchill is not completely unjustified.
3 Emma has been led to believe that she is cleverer than she really is. She has always been allowed her own way by Miss Taylor, who will not accept Mr Knightley's criticism of her charge. Mr Woodhouse thinks Emma can do no wrong and believes Harriet is as good a friend for Emma as Jane Fairfax would have been.
4 Emma lives a very lonely life. Her sister lives far away and Miss Taylor has left Hartfield to marry. Her only companion at home is her father, who is tedious company.
5 Mr Elton's only motive for being pleasant to Harriet is to curry favour with Emma, whom he wants to marry because of her wealth. His proposal to Emma shows little real feeling, and he soon marries someone else on very short acquaintance.
6 Emma encourages Harriet to give up a perfectly good offer of marriage. She enjoys her friend's company simply because she can tell her what to think. Harriet flatters Emma's sense of her own importance. Mr Knightley, who understands Emma well, believes the friendship to be a bad thing.
7 Everyone in Highbury is carefully placed in his or her social position by author and characters alike. Mrs and Miss Bates and Mrs Goddard are described as being from 'a second set'. Mr Knightley draws a distinction between Harriet and Robert Martin. Mr Elton believes that 'everyone has their level'.

8   Like her father, Isabella is obsessed by the concerns of her own family. She follows the orders of her own doctor as Mr Woodhouse follows the orders of Mr Perry.

9   Everything we hear about Robert Martin attests to his kindness and good nature. Mr Knightley, who always shows good judgement, supports his suit.

10   We have enough evidence to show that Frank could have come to Highbury. He has been in Weymouth. His excuses for not coming sound lame and Mr Knightley sees through them.

What is the significance?

1   Mr Woodhouse, in Chapter 1, about Mr Knightley's walk to Hartfield. This is a typical example of Mr Woodhouse's fearful attitude towards bad weather.

2   Harriet Smith, in Chapter 4, describing Robert Martin. This is one of the first examples of Harriet's inability to make up her mind.

3   Mr Knightley, in Chapter 5, speaking of his fears concerning the friendship between Harriet and Emma. This is an example of Mr Knightley's witty, epigrammatic style.

4   Emma, thinking about Mr Elton in Chapter 6. This is one of the first signs of doubt in Emma's mind concerning Mr Elton's intentions towards Harriet. Rather typically, Emma ignores her doubts. Emma, like Mr Knightley, expresses herself in witty style.

5   Mr Knightley to Emma in Chapter 8, concerning the advice Emma has given to Harriet to turn down Robert Martin's proposal. This is the first time we see Mr Knightley angry with Emma. The coolness between them lasts for some time and is not fully resolved until he proposes to her.

6   Emma speaking about Mr Elton in Chapter 9. Emma prides herself on her ability to interpret riddles, but cannot interpret Mr Elton's actions.

7   Emma to Harriet in Chapter 10, concerning her intention to remain single. Emma cannot even predict her own actions accurately.

8   Mr Weston speaking about Mrs Churchill in Chapter 14. Mr Weston always uses quite strong language to express his dislike of Mrs Churchill, presumably because of the part she played in souring his first marriage. She is the only person to receive such treatment from this very amiable man.

9   Mr Elton speaking dismissively of Harriet when proposing to Emma in Chapter 15.

10   Mr Knightley speaking of Frank Churchill in Chapter 18. Frank is one of the few people to be spoken of unkindly by Mr Knightley. We eventually realise that the main reason for this is jealousy.

■ Self-test answers Chapters 19–36 (Volume 2)

Who? What? Why? When? Where? How?

1   Jane was adopted by Colonel Campbell, a friend of her father's. Colonel Campbell felt he owed a debt of gratitude to Jane's father, a fellow officer, who had helped him when he was sick.

2   Emma thinks that Jane is too reserved and rather cold. She is a little jealous of Jane's musical accomplishment and does not enjoy being compared with her.

3   Emma decides the visit is a necessary evil as it will serve to take Harriet's mind off Mr Elton's engagement.
4   On his first walk around the village of Highbury, the sight of the Crown Inn suggests the idea to Frank.
5   At the Coles' dinner party.
6   Mrs Weston suggests that Mr Knightley may be in love with Jane Fairfax.
7   Frank Churchill.
8   Frank is recalled to Enscombe.
9   At Maple Grove, near Bristol.
10 Mrs Elton presses Jane to take up a post as governess.

Prove it
1   In Chapter 20, we hear that Jane was given 'an excellent education' by 'first-rate masters'. She has enjoyed 'all the rational pleasures of an elegant society.' Emma has rarely travelled from Highbury and was educated only by Miss Taylor.
2   When Mr Knightley tells Emma about the engagement he smiles, 'which implied a conviction of some part of what had passed between them.'
3   Frank makes up an excuse for visiting the Bates household on his first day in Highbury and finds pretexts for frequent visits thereafter. On one occasion he persuades Mrs Weston she had said she intended to visit them.
4   When Emma considers snubbing the Coles in Chapter 25, she realises they would not support her. 'This lesson, she very much feared, they would receive only from herself; she had little hope of Mr Knightley, none of Mr Weston.'
5   After dinner at the Coles, in Chapter 27, Emma 'did unfeignedly and unequivocally regret the inferiority of her own playing and singing. She did most heartily grieve over the idleness of her childhood – and sat down and practised vigorously for half an hour.'
6   In Chapter 29, as they plan the ball, Frank asks Emma to dance the first two dances with him and Mr and Mrs Weston look on in approval, "He has asked her, my dear. That's right. I knew he would."
7   By the time Frank leaves for Enscombe, and the ball is cancelled, Jane has already been embarrassed by the gift of the piano and has watched Frank toy with Emma's affections. She must wonder whether the man who cannot choose to attend a ball will ever be allowed to marry the woman of his choice.
8   Mrs Elton is over-dressed and overbearing. She refers to men by their surnames without a title, and to women by their Christian name; she calls her husband 'Mr E.' or 'Caro sposo' (adopting an unacceptable informality by the standards of the time and being insufferably trendy). She brags about her connections: in Chapter 32 she refers to Maple Grove seven times, to her brother-in-law's barouche-landau three times and to Bath four times.
9   In Chapter 34 we are told of Mr John Knightley's meeting with Jane Fairfax while on a morning walk with his little boys, which shows he spends time with his sons. At dinner he makes a note of Mrs Elton's clothes so he can inform his wife and has kind wishes for Jane Fairfax's future.
10 In Chapter 36, Mrs Elton betrays the information that her brother-in-law has lived at Maple Grove for a mere eleven years and that there is some doubt that his father had completed the purchase of the house before his death. This is in contrast to the Knightleys and the Woodhouses who have lived on their estates for generations.

What is the significance?
1   Miss Bates to Emma in Chapter 19. This is when Emma first conceives of the fantasy of an affair between Jane and Mr Dixon.

2   Harriet to Emma in Chapter 22 after meeting Robert Martin at Ford's. This exchange demonstrates Harriet's willingness to be ruled by Emma.

3   Frank Churchill to Emma in Chapter 23. Frank shows his ability to speak well of everyone in order to please his listener.

4   Emma, questioning Frank in Chapter 24. Frank steps into Ford's to buy himself time before answering this question. He is wary of revealing his involvement with Jane.

5   Chapter 25, Mr Woodhouse speaking of the Coles' planned dinner party. As usual, Emma experiences difficulty in arranging a night out.

6   Frank Churchill to Emma, in Chapter 26, speaking of Jane Fairfax. As usual, Frank is engaging in double-dealing, indulging in gossip with Emma while making excuses to talk to Jane.

7   Mr Knightley to Emma in Chapter 30, during a conversation about the forthcoming ball. Here, Mr Knightley is behaving like a confirmed bachelor, a state of mind that is soon to change.

8   Mrs Elton to Emma on her first visit to Hartfield in Chapter 32, making her first opportunity to refer to Maple Grove.

9   Mr Knightley to Emma upon being told of speculation that he is in love with Jane in Chapter 33. These rumours have obviously awakened unbachelor-like emotions in Mr Knightley.

10   Emma replying to John Knightley's accusations, in Chapter 36, that an increased social life will leave her little time for her nephews. Emma clearly has little fun and is in danger of becoming a maiden aunt.

■ Self-test questions Chapters 37–55 (Volume 3)

Who? What? Why? When? Where? How?

1   The Churchills.

2   'To be the favourite and intimate of a man who had so many favourites and confidantes, was not the very first distinction in the scale of vanity.'

3   To rescue her from the embarrassment of being snubbed by Mr Elton.

4   Mid-June.

5   Emma told her she would have to limit herself to saying only three very dull things.

6   Mrs Smallridge, an acquaintance of Mrs Suckling.

7   Frank has been secretly engaged to Jane since meeting her in Weymouth.

8   Ostensibly to stay with Isabella in order to go to the dentist, but really to help her to forget Mr Knightley.

9   Robert Martin wins back her affection. He calls at Brunswick Square and, after a trip to the theatre and dinner, proposes to Harriet once more.

10   He decides he needs Mr Knightley's protection after a series of thefts.

Prove it

1   During the ball, she hopes he is watching her dancing. She admires the way he rescued Harriet. She dances with him, saying, "We are not really so much brother and sister as to make it at all improper."

2 When she believes it is Mrs Cole at the door she says, "It must be borne some time or other, and it may as well be now." When she realises it is Emma she refuses to see her, probably because of the way Emma had treated her aunt and flirted with Frank.

3 Miss Bates tells Emma that Jane spoke to Mrs Elton about the post after a call from John, the ostler. He had mentioned that Frank had set off for Richmond.

4 He is more concerned about the fact that Mr Knightley is setting off for London – Jane's news 'interested without disturbing him.'

5 Emma tells herself 'she would not marry, even if she were asked by Mr Knightley'.

6 He returns from London to comfort her. He says, "Time will heal the wound." He calls Frank, "An abominable scoundrel."

7 In Chapter 51, 'She found amusement in detecting the real cause of that violent dislike of Mr Knightley's marrying Jane Fairfax.'

8 When he is told of Emma's engagement, he agrees to keep it secret but tells Jane the next day. 'It was no more than the principals were prepared for.'

9 In Chapter 54, he teases Jane about the blunder over Mr Perry's carriage, "I see it in her cheek, her smile, her vain attempt to frown." Both Emma and Jane take the memory of these misunderstandings more seriously.

10 When she returned from London in Chapter 55, she 'owned that she had been presumptuous and silly and self-deceived.'

What is the significance?

1 Frank Churchill to Emma in Chapter 38, at the ball. He is not really interested in Mrs Elton but in Jane, who is to arrive in the Eltons' carriage.

2 Mr Elton to Harriet at the ball in Chapter 38. He is snubbing Harriet to get his own back on Emma for turning down his proposal.

3 Emma to Harriet in Chapter 41 as they discuss Harriet's new love. Emma is referring to Frank Churchill who rescued Harriet from the gypsies, but Harriet has been talking of Mr Knightley dancing with her at the ball.

4 This is the word that Frank puts before Jane when they are playing word games in Chapter 41. This word, and the reference to Mr Perry's carriage, cause Mr Knightley to suspect that there is something between Jane and Frank.

5 This is Mrs Elton's pretentious idea of elegant simplicity, in Chapter 42, as she attempts to plan Mr Knightley's strawberry party.

6 In Chapter 45, after the trip to Box Hill when Jane is ill, Emma tries to help her in a number of ways but all offers of food and a ride in the carriage are rejected. After refusing the carriage, Jane is seen walking and Emma realises that Jane resents her offers of help.

7 Emma to Mrs Weston, in Chapter 46, on hearing that Frank and Jane are to be married. Emma's sympathetic reaction to Jane's plight and her condemnation of Frank's behaviour show her increased understanding and empathy for Jane. Now she is thinking like Mr Knightley.

8 Harriet to Emma, in Chapter 47, explaining that she is in love with Mr Knightley. In preferring Mr Knightley, Harriet is showing more discrimination than Emma has done up until this moment.

9 Mr Knightley proposing to Emma in Chapter 49. This rather reticent love scene is typical of Austen's style.

10 In Chapter 55, the irrepressible Mrs Elton has the last word on Emma's wedding, revealing her vulgarity to the last.

Notes

Notes

Notes